Zacharias Tanee Fomum

THE WAY
OF VICTORIOUS
PRAYING

Éditions du Livre Chrétien
4, rue du Révérend Père Cloarec
92400 Courbevoie France
editionlivrechretien@gmail.com

The way of victorious praying

First Edition
Published by Vantage Press, Inc. New York.
ISBN: 0-533-07884-9
Library of Congress Catalogue Card no. 87-90351

Published by :
Editions du livre chrétien
4, rue du Révérend Père Cloarec
92400 Courbevoie - FRANCE
Tél : (33) 9 52 29 27 72
Email : editionlivrechretien@gmail.com

Cover :
Jacques Maré

I gladly dedicate this book to

The Fasting Intercessors for Cameroon

In grateful appreciation
for their nation-transforming praying

Table of contents

Preface

This book was born out of prayer. The Lord called a few of us aside to pray. Each night, we wrestled in prayer between the hours of 9:00 P.M and 3:00 A.M. This went on for many weeks. We came to find ourselves blessed, challenged, and purified. We came to see the Lord in a new way and to understand the purpose of our being in a totally new light.

This book was also born out of an experience – an experience of obedience. Some of us were led to obey an obvious command of the Lord, which is clearly written in the Bible and which we had not yet obeyed. That obedience nearly cost us our lives. God honoured that obedience and caused it to lead to the ministries now associated with Christian Literature Centre, Yaoundé. It also led to the birth of some assemblies which have, by God's grace, grown into praying communities.

The truths charted in this book are coloured by what that local assembly has learnt as it tried, step by step, to follow the praying Lord in the School of Prayer. We have a commitment to prayer, fasting, and evangelism. We are learning and we are growing. Pray for us. Pray with us.

We have come to discover that all things are possible to the praying saint and to the praying body of believers. By God's grace, we are determined to wipe out the word "impossible" from the life experience of the members of the assembly.

Our hearts' desire is that all those who know the Lord Jesus will truly become people of prayer. So we send this book out with prayer that it will help some individuals and some local assemblies to make progress with the Lord in the "School of Prayer".

To the Lord Jesus, the praying, supplicating and interceding Head of the Church be untold honour, glory, and majesty forever and ever.

Zacharias Tanee Fomum
July 1984
Yaoundé Cameroon

CHAPTER 1

What is prayer ?

Prayer takes place when a believer's will takes the same side with God's will to worship Him, thank and praise Him, and ask as well as receive from Him. This taking sides with God's will in the human spirit is expressed actively and vocally. Prayer is the art of soul being lost in God-adoring and worshiping Him. It is the insistence that God's will, which has already been established in heaven, should be done. Prayer is the commitment of a believer to fulfil and to satisfy the needs of God. Prayer is the rail on which the locomotive of God's will moves.

HEAVEN GOVERNED BY EARTH

God has a will and all the power needed to execute that will unaided by man. However, in His sovereignty, He has decided that, unless He finds people who will co-operate with Him by praying. He will temporarily let His will go unaccomplished. The Bible says, *"Truly, I say to you, whatever you bind on earth shall be, having been bound in heaven and whatever you loose on earth shall be, having been loosed in heaven"* (Matthew 18:18-19). Heaven has already bound and heaven has already loosed. What then must happen before this thing that has been bound or loosed can become practical reality on earth? It is this: earth must bind and earth must loose. Without this, what has been done in heaven will be forced to wait. God will allow a lot of His resolutions to go unfulfilled for some time if He does not find people to co-operate with Him in prayer.

God will postpone His work or allow it to appear as if He did not care about it, until He finds someone who can pray and who does pray. He will allow a nation to go through many years without much happening until He finds His man – a man of prayer, and then He will move in a very might way.

God will temporarily allow the devil to win many battles if He does not find people who will co-operate with Him to overthrow the devil and put the armies of hell to flight.

PRAYING PEOPLE

Prayer calls for people who are totally consecrated to the Lord, because only such people are able to know God's will and God's needs. Such saints have it as their ambition to fulfil God's needs. Their one desire is that God's will in its totality be accomplished on earth. Only consecrated people can truly pray, for they are people who have forgotten themselves in the accomplishment of God's will. The Lord Jesus taught that the foremost things in prayer were to be "*Hallowed be Thy name. Thy Kingdom come; Thy will be done on earth as it is in heaven*" (Matthew 6:9-10). This is the crux of prayer, the very essence of prayer. Prayer is the complete abandonment to God with only one concern – that His name be hallowed and His will be done. This makes prayer very holy business, and only the holy can go deep in prayer fellowship with the Holy God.

Exploiters, that is people whose main business is to get things out of God for their selfish motives, will find deep prayer impossible, for their whole desire is, "God, give me this and this and that."

ASKING AND RECEIVING

Prayer is asking and receiving from the Lord, His perfect will and the accomplishment of that will. The Lord Jesus said: "*Ask and you shall receive.*" To ask and not to receive is a very serious affair that must not be taken lightly at all. If a believer asks something from the Lord and does not receive it, he should consider it a signal of spiritual danger. Prayer is not only asking and receiving things that are exclusively for the Kingdom. It includes the asking today for the meal of tomorrow. The Lord Jesus said, "*Seek ye first the Kingdom of God and His righteousness and all these other things shall be added unto you*" (Matthew 6:33).

If a man's heart is right with regard to God and His perfect will, his priorities will not be his daily needs but the Lord's will. He will judge everything by the way it affects the will of God. Even his personal needs will be reassessed in light of the King. He will live to see God's Kingdom established. He will dress, eat, study, and marry for the Kingdom. He will have one unchanging yardstick by which he judges everything: "Is this of God or of the devil and will this build the Kingdom of God or retard it?" It is a tragedy to pray for things that retard the Kingdom of God, but oh, how many are the sons of the Kingdom who pray that way !

PRAYER A RAIL

Prayer is the rail on which the train of God's power moves. A huge locomotive with and appropriately big engine will not move even for the shortest distance if there are no rails on which it can move. God, in His wondrous sovereignty, has decided to limit Himself to the rails that the Church provides for Him. The more the rails of prayer that the Church makes available, the more the locomotive of God's power will move. The fewer the rails that are made available, the less the locomotive of the power of the Lord will move. The lesser men pray, the lesser God will move. We know in this local assembly that one tract had led four people to the Lord because the Church prays. In this local assembly, if the prayer life were tripled, God's power train would have three times more rails to move on and one tract would lead twelve people to the Lord, and if the Church prayed one hundredfold, one tract would lead four hundred people to Christ. I believe that we can increase our prayer life one hundredfold and that must be our goal.

PRAYER IS CONFLICT

Under normal circumstances prayer would be simply asking from the Lord as a child asks from his father thus, "Daddy, give me X or Y, " and receiving the answer from him without straining, agonizing or pressing on. This indeed is true for certain aspects of prayer and some occasions. However, in many instances this is not so. We have to strain, agonize, and press on in order to obtain what we want from the Lord. Why is this so? Why this struggle?

The reason for the struggle lies in the very nature of who is involved or affected by prayer. Prayer involves three persons. There is the person praying, there is God to whom the prayer is being addressed, and there is the third person who many ignore to their undoing. He is the Enemy, Satan, who opposes, hinders, and delays prayer. Prayer, therefore, is violent opposition to the will of the devil. It is merciless destruction of his cause and his army. Prayer is hard work. It is violent activity. The more praying there is, the more the devil is put out of control. The less the praying, the less his cause is hindered. The devil has so much authority today in the world because of the many spectators in the Church who do not pray or who pray too little.

The conflict with the wicked one means that prayer will sometimes involve cries, tears, groans, agony, heartache, and wrestling. Deep prayer is conflict, expensive conflict! How sad it is to know that only very few of God's children know anything about this!!

May we grow up and face the fight in prayer! May we develop a holy anger towards the enemy. May we say, "Satan, I am going to deal with you. In the name of Jesus I come against you and your kingdom and I do not spare it."

Prayer is persisting work

Some believers pray one or two times, or for one or two years, and when they do not see the answer, they are discouraged and say, "God has not answered. Hallelujah." If after praying for an unbeliever for four or five years and he is not converted; if the praying person gives up, it reflects the fact that he was never serious at all. God will answer. Sometimes He will answer before we call. In other instances, He will answer long after we have called. If we are in His will, there can be no giving up of a topic of prayer until the answer has been given. Those who think that prayer is modern computerized science in which you fit in the data, press a button, and have the answer have missed it completely.

When the Lord Jesus taught on persistence in prayer, He said, *"Nevertheless when the Son of man comes, will he find faith on earth?"* Why did He ask that question? It is this: the person with genuine faith is the one who can enter into real prayer. The sad thing is that if the Lord came today, He would find very few with genuine faith. Those with genuine faith are not the "magicians" who just want to say, "In the name of Jesus, stand and walk." They are wrestlers who will put everything into the fight and never give up. Peter and John could say, *"In the name of Jesus, stand up and walk"* (Acts 3:6). But let us remember that these were praying men from a praying Church.

So as we approach prayer, let us bear in mind that it is a total business for a total people.

As we study this subject, may the Holy Spirit who prays for us with groans too deep for words and our interceding High Priest, the Lord Jesus, stand by us to reveal His truth to us, and to lead us on. Glory be to the Lord in the highest. Amen.

WHAT IS PRAYERLESSNESS

Prayerlessness is the refusal to take up the mighty weapons of prayer and be involved with God in His battles. Prayerlessness is too little or no effective praying. Prayerlessness is absolute rebellion. It is the deliberate refusal to obey God's command to pray. Prayerlessness is a great sin. It is a determination to take an active side with the devil to fight against God. It is a determination to frustrate God's purposes, to wreck the Kingdom of God.

Prayerlessness is a determined effort to ensure that sinners are lost in hell forevermore. It is a calculated effort to ensure that backsliders are not restored and that ultimate victory should belong to the wicked one.

All who do not pray make themselves enemies of the praying Lord. If souls are lost, it is because there are prayerless believers, for no soul is won into the Kingdom of God unless the price has been paid in terms of vital praying. Every soul that is lost to the deil is lost because the Church did not pray at all or did not pray effectively. Prayerless believers will answer to the Lord on Judgement Day for all the souls that have perished forevermore. They are guilty of the blood of these people.

Fellow saint, the worst sin you can commit as a child of God is to pray superficially or not to pray at all. Prayerlessness is high treason against the government of God. It is betraying God and the entire cause of the Kingdom of God. Prayerlessness is the fool's way of life, the sluggard's companion, and the way to a life of planned spiritual darkness and poverty.

You dare not allow yourself the luxury of so great a sin!!!

Think about the conversion of Saul, who later on became the apostle Paul. Some people think that it just happened. Such people do not imagine how many people prayed for this one man who was terrorizing the Church. Each time the believers met, they must have prayed for him. Because they prayed, God brought him to conversion and regeneration. Saul would never have been converted without the prayers of the Church. Praying churches are living churches, and living churches are growing churches.

If there is a thing that should be done now for the glory of God, it is to pray. I encourage everyone to pray and to rally men to prayer. Dare not stand to lead a prayer meeting, to pray or sing for the Lord, without an active life of prayer. Dare not preach to men about God until you have told God about men in prayer. If you preach without much prayer you frustrate God's purposes. Please, again I say, "Pray."

CHAPTER 2

The Lord Jesus at prayer

The Lord Jesus was given to prayer. He prayed. His life and ministry began in prayer, continued in prayer, and was consummated in prayer. Right at the tender age of twelve years He remained in the temple, and when His anxious parents saw Him and questioned, He simply asked, *"How is it that you sought me? Did you not know that I must be in my Father's house ?"* (Luke 2:49). He was in His Father's house – the house of prayer (Mark 11:17) and it goes without question that He must have prayed.

Later on, he was baptized in water by John the Baptist, He immediately began to pray and as He prayed, the Holy Spirit came upon Him. The Bible says, *"Now when all the people were baptized, and when Jesus also had been baptized AND WAS PRAYING, the heavens opened, ant the Holy spirit descended upon Him"* (Luke 3:21,22).

He prayed as a way of life. The Bible says, *"And in the morning, a great while before day, He rose and went out to a lonely place, AND THERE HE PRAYED"* (Mark 1:35). Prayer was the first business of the Lord. He decided not to see the face of man before He had seen the face of His Father, and not to talk to men about His Father until He had talked to His Father about men.

Faced with the crucial issue of choosing the twelve apostles, He found that such a far-reaching decision required much time with His Father beyond the normal mornings spent in prayer. So He spent the whole night in prayer. The Bible says, *"In these days He went out to the mountain to pray; and ALL NIGHT HE CONTINUED IN PRAYER TO GOD. And when it was day, He called His disciples, and chose from them twelve, whom He named apostles"* (Luke 6:12-13). That was the Lord's way of handling big and far-reaching decisions.

The Lord was always at prayer. He often withdrew to lonely places and there prayed alone. The Bible says, *"Now it happened that as He was praying alone the disciples were with Him"* (Luke 9:18); *"Now about eight days after these sayings He took with Him Peter and John and James, and went up on the mountain to pray. And as He was praying, the appearance of His countenance was altered, and His raiment became dazzling white"* (Luke 9:28-29); *"But He withdrew to the wilderness and prayed"* (Luke 5:16). *"Immediately He made His disciples get into the boat and go before Him to the other side, to Bethsaida, while He dismissed the crowd. And after He had taken leave of them, He went up on the mountain to pray"* (Mark 6:45-46). *"Then Jesus went with them to a place called Gethsemane, and He said to His disciples, 'Sit here, while I go yonder and pray'. And taking with Him Peter and the two sons of Zebedee, He began to be sorrowful and troubled. Then He said to hem, 'My soul is very sorrowful, even to death; remain here, and watch with me.' And going a little further He fell on His face and prayed, 'My father'"*... (Matthew 26:36-39).

Jesus knew that deep prayer was a matter between God and the praying person, whom no one should disturb. He thus withdrew so often into lonely places. Often He must have just prayed with His disciples by Him, like during the incident which Luke records by saying, *"He was praying in a certain place, and when He ceased, one of His disciples said to Him, 'Lord, teach us to pray'"* (Luke 11:1). Often He took a few of them away with Him to pray, but the most precious times of His life were His moments alone with God – all others away. He must have enjoyed these so much that He "naturally" just withdrew to have those times with His Father. Although He lived in unceasing fellowship with His Father, He nevertheless delighted in those precious moments when, alone with Him, He could enter into something akin to the fellowship they knew together in heaven before. He came down to earth. Jesus literally lived in expectation of those times of fellowship in prayer. They meant everything to Him

All people who pray will normally enjoy fellowship with God all the time, but they will so know God and so enjoy Him that general times of fellowship will not fully satisfy. They, therefore, look for privacy with Him. They will withdraw from the world to be with Him. They long for Him and languish for Him and are unsatisfied until He fills them.

So we see that for Jesus, prayer was, first of all, not a matter of asking and receiving. It was communion, fellowship. It was enjoying God. It was heart fellowship.

Secondly, prayer for Jesus served to obtain guidance. He knew He had to appoint twelve of His many disciples as apostles. Possibly, He already knew in His heart who was likely to be appointed. He was very God of very God, but He still went apart to ask the Father, to check with Him. He spent the whole night, as it were, going from one name to the other, asking the Father's approval. The Father gave His approval and He came and made the appointments and the consequence of who was appointed spans time and eternity!.

Thirdly, prayer for Jesus was a matter of warfare. He knew the Father's will. He also knew the Enemy's commitment to thwart that will. He reinforced the Father's will against the devil's will; He engaged in mighty conflict with the devil in prayer, His sweat becoming like drops of blood as He prayed the Father's will through to victory. So throughout His whole life, each time He saw a violent attack on the Father's will, He went aside to pray until the tide of the Enemy's activity subsided.

Fourthly, the prayer life of the Lord was one of mighty, potent intercession. He just interceded. From the moment when He selected the apostles and called them apart, He must have interceded for them as individuals and as a team. How He must have interceded for Peter! He Himself said, *"Simon, Simon, behold, Satan demanded to have you, that he might sift you like wheat but I HAVE PRAYED FOR YOU that your faith may not fail; and when you have turned again, strengthen you brethren"* (Luke 22:31-32). Peter was truly tested and he even failed, but he repented and went on. Had Jesus not interceded for him, he would have failed utterly. The contribution of Peter to the Church depended not so much on Peter as on the Lord who called him, and in his hour of deepest weakness prayed for him. The intercessory ministry of the Lord is of such importance that it is one of the ministries that He carries out right from the throne of all glory.

Fifthly, prayer for Jesus was importunity. It is not that He doubted God's love and willingness to do things. He just knew that something wonderful happened in the spiritual realm when the praying person held on to his request and persisted in prayer. He engaged in this aspect of prayer when, at Gethsemane, He prayed not only once or twice but thrice about "the cup." This was importunity by the Lord. His prayer was in the Father's will, yet He importuned God. What an example!.

Sixthly, prayer to Jesus was a matter of watching. He told the disciples to watch and pray. He must certainly have been saying it from deep experience. He watched and prayed so much that He insisted upon it. *He said, "Watch and pray that you may not enter into temptation. The spirit is willing but the flesh is weak" (Matthew 26:41). The Lord asked the sleeping disciples, "So, could you not watch with me one hour?"* (Matthew 26:40) He Himself was obviously watching and was sad that His closest disciples could not watch with Him.

The seventh thing that prayer was to Jesus was that it provided the mechanism for asking and receiving things from the Father. He asked the Father that Lazarus be raised from the dead and the Father answered Him in the affirmative (John 11:41-44). He asked the Father to glorify Him. His actual prayer was, *"Father, the hour has come; glorify the Son that the Son may glorify Thee... I glorified Thee on earth, having accomplished the work which Thou gavest me to do; and now, Father, glorify Thou me in Thy own presence with the glory which I had with Thee before the world was made"* (John 17:1-5). The Father also answered this prayer for the apostle Peter, who in talking of the resurrected Lord said, *"The God of our fathers raised Jesus whom you killed by hanging on the tree. God exalted Him at His right hand as the Leader and Saviour"* (Acts 5:30,31). Jesus received answers to all the prayers He ever made because He fulfilled all the requirements of God for prayer to be answered.

The eighth thing about the prayer life of the Lord Jesus was that He prayed for the Church. He prayed like this, *"I have given them Thy word; and the world has hated them because they are not of the world, even as I am not of the world. I do not pray that Thou shouldst take them out of the world, but that Thou shouldst keep them from the evil one. They are not of the world, even as I am not of the world. Sanctify then in the truth, Thy word is truth. As Thou didst send me into the world, so I have sent them into the world. And for their sake, I consecrate myself, so that they may be consecrated in truth., I do not pray for these only, but also for those who believe in me through their word, that they may be one; even as Thou, Father, art in me, and I in Thee, that they also may be in us, so that the world may believe that Thou hast sent me"* (John 17:14-21).

The ninth thing about the prayer life of the Lord Jesus is that He supplicated. He prayed deeply in dead earnest. The Bible says about Him that, *"In the days of His flesh, Jesus offered up prayers and supplications, with loud cries and tears, to Him who was able to save Him from death, and He was heard for His godly fear"* (Hebrews 5:7).

The tenth thing about the prayer life of the Lord Jesus was that He taught people to pray and commanded people to pray. He said to His disciples, *"When you pray, say: Father, hallowed be Thy name. Thy Kingdom come…"* (Luke 11:2-13). He encouraged them to pray for labourers, for He said to them, *"The harvest is plentiful, but the labourers are few; pray therefore the Lord of the harvest to send out labourers into His harvest"* (Matthew 9:37-38). The Lord did not only pray. He wanted people to pray. His concern today is that in addition to praying men, there be some of them who, in addition to praying, call and teach others to pray and to reproduce teachers of the holy art of prayer.

The eleventh thing about the prayer life of the Lord Jesus was that He saw that prayer and fasting were mutual companions. He Himself fasted and prayed. His disciples fasted and prayed, and the victorious Church continues to be a fasting, praying Church.

The last thing we would like to say about the prayer life of the Lord is that His earthly life so lived in the power of prayer was terminated in prayer. His last words were a prayer, *"'Father, into Thy hands I commit my spirit' and having said this, He breathed His last"* (Luke 23:46). Before this last act of worship and prayer, He had clearly shown that prayer would be answered only if it fulfilled the required conditions set out by God.

Jesus is, thus, our supreme example of prayer. We do well to follow Him into the School of Prayer and sit at His feet to be taught by Him. My prayer today is that some people will again confess their ignorance on how to pray and turn to Him, the Lord of glory, and ask Him again, "Lord, teach us how to pray." If they do so, by the power of the indwelling Lord, the Holy Spirit will help us in our weakness and ignorance, teach us, intercede for us, and make us into people who can teach others the art of holy praying.

CHAPTER 3

Prayer :

A spiritual conflict

THE DEVIL'S ATTACK ON PRAYER AND THE BELIEVERS'S WAY OF VICTORY

We have said that there are two master wills in conflict - the will of the Eternal Father and the will of the Prince of Darkness - and that God in His sovereignty will temporarily allow His purposes to go unaccomplished and the wicked one to apparently win, if believers, by an active decision of their wills, do not take sides with God's will by prayer. In that sense, then, the prayer of God's children becomes the greatest opposition to the cause of the Enemy that could be. Because this is so, the devil has marshalled a tremendous force, using his total trinity of the devil, the flesh, and the world to attack prayer. If he wins there, he has won. If, on the other hand, the Church wins, then the devil's cause suffers tragic but glorious ruin. Let us look now at his attack on prayer, and then we shall turn to the way of victory since the Church has no choice but to win. God is ultimately undefeatable.

THE DEVIL'S ATTACK ON PRAYER

The Restless Destroyer

The Enemy once told the Eternal Father, in response to a question, "Whence have you come?" that he had come "From going to and fro on the earth, and from walking up and down on it" (Job 1:7). He is the god of this world and he is not sleeping or resting. He is far from taking a holiday. If some believers are resting or on holiday, I call them to awaken to the fact that the devil takes no holidays. He never sleeps. He goes "to and fro, up and down." We may ask, What is he up to? Why does he go all over? The apostle Peter gives us the answer. He says, "Your adversary the devil prowls around like a roaring lion, seeking some one to devour" (I Peter 5:8). He moves up and down so that he may prowl very near and be ready to attack at the slightest opening. Whom does he want to attack? He principally wants to attack believers with regards to prayer - to cause them either not to pray or, if they insist, to cause them not to pray victoriously. This is his master strategy.

I humbly plead with all of God's children to see with me that the whole world has not been evangelized up to now, and the Church has not been rendered spotless and without blemish, because the devil has scored some very great victories here in fighting against prayer. May God open our eyes to the fact that the central victory with regards, to world evangelism is not speakers and evangelists, needful as these are, but prayer. The Lord is not going to come to satisfy the desires of speculators about the last days but to fulfil the desires of His lovers who usher His return and reign by prayer. The Enemy is at work. Will the Church rise to prayer? Every area of prayer – intercession, supplication, fasting - is being attacked by the Enemy. May God open our eyes to this fact and may He teach us how to counter these attacks. Satan is restless. May we, too, become restless. He wants to destroy us. May we destroy him beforehand.

Destruction through Ignorance

The Lord said that His people perished for want of knowledge. The ignorance of the average believer, of the Word of God, the way of victory, the life of prayer, et cetera, is amazing. The devil is at the root of this. He blinds believers!!!

He blinds believers from knowing that they have access to the Father through the blood of the Son. He emphasizes the fact that they have sinned and if they come to the Lord in prayer, He will not hear them. He causes some believers to carry an unending sense of guilt over sins that have been confessed and forgiven, and sometimes he causes guilt over sins that have not been committed at all. Where there is no sin yet, he causes the believer to feel that he will soon commit a terrible sin and so should not pray. He suggests to those who have sinned that it is not necessary to confess their sin at once. God is still too angry with them to hear them. They should allow some time to go by so that God's anger should cool down and maybe they will then the able to confess and be heard. Sometimes he tells some believers not to bother about confessing but to just wait, for time will heal the wounds caused by their sin and God will forget with time. All this is aimed and destroying the grounds of assurance by which we come to the Father. The Word of God says, *"For we have not a high priest who is unable to sympathize with our weaknesses, but one who in every respect has been tempted as we are, yet without sin. LET US THEN WITH CONFIDENCE DRAW NEAR TO THE THRONE OF GRACE, THAT WE MAY RECEIVE MERCY AND FIND GRACE TO HELP IN TIME OF NEED" (Hebrews 4:15-16). "FOR THROUGH HIM WE BOTH HAVE ACCESS IN ONE SPIRIT TO THE FATHER"* (Ephesians 2:18). If the devil is accusing you because of a sin you have committed, confess the sin, forsake it and then quote the following scripture to Satan when he next comes, *"If we confess our sins, He is faithful and just, and will forgive our sins and cleanse us from all unrighteousness"* (1 John 1:9). After that say to him, "Shame, Satan. Depart from me."

He may attack by causing us to doubt the faithfulness of God. He may say, "Think of this issue about which you have prayed and prayed and yet there is no answer. God does not answer the prayers of everybody. He has his favourites. You are not one of them. Don't bother to pray because you will not get anything out of it." To this, you can simply open your prayer record that you have received. Remind him that God has asked you to continue in prayer over some issues and that this is one of them. Tell the devil that you are God's favourite and therefore God's best is for you. Quote the following scripture to him. It is God talking about your being special and precious to Him: *"Because you are precious in My eyes, and honoured, and I love you, I give men in return for you, peoples in exchange for your life"* (Isaiah 43:4). Remind him of all God's promises to answer prayer. Quote them to him one after another, and then tell him to be gone.

He may attack in a more dangerous way by saying that you do not need to pray, that prayer is for weak people or for people who are unable. He may suggest that you are very well able and even suggest to you all the potentials that you have for succeeding without prayer. He may quote the names of many unbelievers who have accomplished great things without prayer. This is a most dangerous temptation. It is an invitation to doubt God and trust yourself. It is an invitation to rebellion. Satan is simply saying to you, "Rebel as I did. Declare your independence from God." The first reaction of this is to speak boldly and authoritatively to him to go away. Confess the fact that without God you can do nothing. The Lord Jesus said, "*Apart from me you can do nothing*" (John 15:5). Refuse to rebel. Tell him that all your abilities are from the Lord and that they can best function only in submission to Him. About the success of the unbelievers, quote the following scripture to him, "*Fret not yourself because of the wicked, be not envious of wrongdoers! For they will soon fade like grass, and wither like green herb*" (Psalms 37:1-2).

In another way, he may tempt you to independence by telling you that you may, if you insist, pray about the big issues, but you should not bother God with the small ones. He will suggest that you should, in so acting, prove that you are mature and God can depend on you. Know that God can only "depend" on those who depend on Him. Tell him that you have no strength or ability of your own for the "small" matters. God is concerned about every hair on you head and none drops without His knowledge. What else could be smaller? Tell him this: "Nothing is small. Nothing is big. God alone is great." Then go ahead and pray about all the minute details of your life. They matter to God. Will you consider me vain? If you do, that is your business; but I want to let you know that a few days ago, I stood full length before a mirror and talked to God about my entire physical body -thanking Him for it and asking His help to make some parts more appealing. That is my God and part of the way I relate to Him.

Physical Attack on Prayer

If the devil fails to convince us not to pray, he will go ahead to make the prayer time as difficult as possible. You know something of that feeling of extreme loneliness and total separation from God that sometimes overwhelms a praying saint. It is as if God had shut you away in another world and Himself ran away from it. It is a feeling that comes from the wicked one, but which sometimes the wicked one uses to disturb and sometimes halt the business of prayer of even maturing saints. We must resist him here too. At such times, I suggest that you pray aloud and shout if need be. Quote a verse about God's unchanging presence like, *"Lo, I am with you always, to the close of the age"* (Matthew 28:20). Quote it aloud to remind yourself of God's promise and therefore of His presence. Quote it to remind the Lord that you need His touch at such a time, and quote it to remind the devil that he has failed. Then go on praying.

He may attack you physical bodies by causing feelings of tiredness even after a lot of rest, by putting you into bad moods, by causing you to be weary without reason, by suddenly taking away your peace so that you cannot easily settle down to that calmness that is necessary for prayer. He may cause the phone to ring loudly and persistently just as you kneel to pray, or he may send somebody to visit you just at the crucial moment. He may bring the thought of something that is very pressing to you, and make you feel that you must do that thing at once or there will be great trouble. He may then say that you should not pray now and that a more conducive time will be at night when everything is quiet. At night he will try to drug you with sleep.

We must see these as the Enemy's ways. We must resist the feeling of tiredness. Jumping up and down will be helpful. We must claim victory over our moods. We must claim our peace from the Lord. After all, the Lord left peace as a legacy for us when He said, *"Peace I leave with you, my peace I give to you; not as the world gives do*

I give to you. Let not your hearts be troubled, neither let them be afraid" (John 14:27). If there is a visitor, we should boldly tell him politely that we are just about to go into prayer and that he should wait or call at another time. Does it sound rude keeping him waiting or sending him away? Well, judge for yourself, but I think that it is enormously ruder to keep God, with whom we made the appointment, waiting or send Him away. We must insist and not postpone the prayer time. Prayer time is one of those things that cannot wait. It must not wait.

A Total Attack by the Enemy

The way in which the Enemy launched a total attack on Job is very instructive. He took away all of Job's wealth and all his children in one day. Later on he took away his health. This was an attack from all angles and in one go. It was meant to force surrender. He still does that today. He will want to do it on praying saints. How does one overcome in such a situation? I want to suggest that it is by persisting regardless of what comes.

However, I want to say that the best results are obtained by attacking him first. Before the Six Day War between Egypt and Israel, I understand that Egypt had far more war planes and could have reduced Israel to nothing. How did Israel win? It won by attacking the enemy planes on the ground before they had time to attack. They hit the Egyptian planes in Egyptian airports before they had time to take off and hit Israel.

I believe with my whole heart, and I know a bit of it from experience, that the safest thing for a believer is to attack the devil before he attacks, to fight the battle with him in his own territory and to be the aggressor.

THE BELIEVER'S WAY OF VICTORY

We have already suggested some ways by which the believer is to react to the attack of the wicked one to ensure that the life of prayer is maintained. One thing is, however, deficient in what was suggested there because it presupposes that the devil has attacked the disciple's life of prayer and therefore the disciple has then to do something about it. As we already said in passing, that kind of warfare is dangerous because it would still end with the devil winning in some battles. We suggested that the best thing was for the battle to be fought in the Enemy's camp to ensure that he suffers any casualties that may and will arise in the battle, to attack the devil first and thus to ground all his effort and plans. We believe that the believer has no substitute for this way of fighting if he wants assured victory.

WATCHING IN PRAYER

Watching is a crucial and indispensable aspect of victorious praying. We believe that the forty days of fasting that preceded the Lord's earthly ministry were spent largely in the ministry of watching in prayer. Later on He commended the same ministry to us in very clear terms. In fact, He commended us to carry it out. He said, *"Watch therefore, for you do not know on what day your Lord is coming. But know this, that if the householder had known in what part of the night the thief was coming, he would have watched and would not have let his house be broken into"* (Matthew 24:42-43). (There is a sense, especially for the subject of prayer in which the thief is the devil who comes to steal and kill and destroy.) *"Watch therefore, for you know neither the day nor the hour"* (Matthew 25:13). *"Watch and pray that you may not enter into temptation; the spirit indeed is willing but the flesh is weak"* (Matthew 26:41). *"But watch at all times, praying that you may have strength to escape all these thing that will take place, and to stand before the Son of man"* (Luke 21:36). *"Take heed, watch and pray for you do not know when the time will come. It is like a man going on a journey, when he leaves home and puts his servants in charge, each with his work, and commands the doorkeeper to watch. Watch therefore for you do not know when the master of the house will come, in the evening, or at midnight, or at cockcrow, or in the morning lest he come suddenly and find you sleeping. AND WHAT I SAY TO YOU I SAY TO ALL: WATCH"* (Mark 13:33-37). Of course these passages apply to watching and waiting our MASTER, the Lord of glory to come. But they are very applicable to us, too, for there is the other master sure, not our master, but the devil, who is prepared to come not for good but for evil. The apostle Paul recommended, *"Continue steadfastly in prayer, being watchful in it with thanksgiving"* (Colossians 4:2). When he outlined the way by which he had accomplished his far-reaching ministry for the Lord Jesus, he included, *"Labours, watching,..."* (2 Corinthians 6:5).

The Lord Jesus called us to watch and pray. The apostle does the same. We have no alternative if we are to remain victorious. Let Peter's example serve as a warning to us. In the garden of Gethsemane, the Lord commanded them to watch and pray so that they might not enter into temptation. They did not obey but slept. Not long from them temptation came and one of those who slept instead of watching yielded to temptation and denied the Lord. Had he obeyed the Lord's instruction and watched and prayed, the story would certainly have been different.

As the clock of God's timing moves towards the close of the age, the devil is going to marshal, and he already has his mightiest weapons against the Church and particularly against those who ignore the command of the Lord to watch.

WHAT IS WATCHING IN PRAYER?

Watching is the condition of being spiritually (and, of course, physically) fully alert and quiet before the Lord so that He may reveal things to you by opening your heart and mind to things which you would otherwise not have seen.

During watching, the Lord opens our "eyes" to see ways by which the devil is planning to attack the will of God in one way or the other. This may include planned attack on the ministry of the Church, our bodies, et cetera, just anything that the adversary may want to hit. I normally watch with my pen and paper by me so that as the Lord shows me the plan of the wicked one I write it down so that I will then know how to counter it.

When that part of watching is over, I discuss with the Lord whether I am to approach it by defensive warfare or by an offensive one. If the Lord asks me to crush him when he attacks, or how best to inform those he wants to attack and so get them ready to defend themselves when he so attacks, if the Lord recommends effective warfare, then I will discuss the plan, strategy, timing, et cetera, with Him. With this finished, my part of watching in relationship to the Enemy attack is finished. I now have enough to pray about.

THE ATTACK OF THE DEVIL IN PRAYER

Normally, the believer labours to be at peace with all men. However, we are never to be at peace with the devil. As long as he continues to occupy even one inch of territory that was won for the Lord Jesus on Calvary, we are to attack him and do him harm. No believer should rest until he or she has personally inflicted many injuries on the devil. Let me ask you a few personal questions. Does the devil bear scars of wounds put on him by you? Are there damaged areas in his territory and schemes that bear testimony of your attack on him? Does he sigh with bitterness and say, "But for so and so, my kingdom would be much stronger?" Of course, the foundations of his kingdom were broken at Calvary by our victorious commander-in-chief, the Lord Jesus, and that can never be repeated. We have, however, the responsibility of pulling down his kingdom. We can pull down and we must pull down because the foundations are already broken.

The foremost weapon to be used against the devil is prayer. When the apostle Paul outlines the believer's armour, he puts the most important weapon last. It is prayer. It is that weapon against *which all of hell is powerless. He says, "Pray at all times in the Spirit, with all prayer and supplication... for all the saints..."* (Ephesians 6:18-19). What do we do in this kind of prayer?

WE ASK AND WE BREAK DOWN

The Lord says, *"Ask of me, and I will make the nations your heritage and the ends of the earth your possession. You shall break them with a rod of iron, and dash them in pieces like a potter's vessel"* (Psalms 2:8-9). We ask the Lord for the nations so that we may bring them to a saving knowledge of the Lord Jesus. To do this, we have to overcome the barrier of the devil who holds them in captivity. So, in prayer and by prayer, we break the devil's kingdom, taking each aspect of that kingdom and, in the name of the Lord, dashing it to pieces. Brethren, the devil's kingdom has a point of weakness. It is a point that is discovered in prayer and to which, by prayer, the believer can actually do much havoc. His kingdom, though apparently strong, is very fragile, provided the right weapons are used. A stone may not be broken with a wooden stick but a hammer will do it easily. May we use the right weapons and we shall find that the devil's kingdom is like a potter's vessel of clay. Even if the clay were strong, it would yield to persistent hammering, especially the hammering that is watered by fasting, praise, and thanksgiving. The persistent hammering of supplications will break it down even in the first blows were not successful.

WE WREAK VENGEANCE AND EXECUTE JUDGEMENT

The Word of God says, *"Let the faithful exult in glory; let them sing for joy on their couches. Let the high praises of God be in their throats and two-edged swords in their hands, to wreak vengeance on the nations and chastisement on the peoples, to bind their kings with chains and their nobles with fetters of iron, to execute on them the judgement written! This is glory for all His faithful ones"* (Psalms 149:5-9).

This is most wonderful. We are to praise and fight at the same time. We are to worship the Lord and punish the devil at the same time. This is time not only for praise. This is time not only for warfare. This is time for praise-thanksgiving-warfare. The believer cannot lose in such a battle. He must win. What does he do while praising and while praying? He is to take up the two-edged sword of prayer against the devil and his allies. He is to pull down the nations that are the devil's allies. He is to bind their kings with chains and their nobles with fetters of iron and to pronounce judgement on them for their sin: and then, because they are bound with chains and therefore under his control, in prayer he is to bring them to a saving knowledge of the Lord! This is for all God's faithful ones. This kind of praying is for all the saints. It is hell breaking. It is heaven building. Remember that the purpose of binding the kings and nobles is to render their desires to do harm against the will of God impossible. It is to ground their actions. The binding in victorious praying is with nothing less than chains and fetters of iron. But the purpose is far greater. It is to bring these bound helpless prisoners to the feet of the Lord Jesus. Fellow saint, you can have kings, presidents, and nobles under your feet by prayer of the right kind. You are meant to have a foretaste of the rulership that will be yours in the Kingdom, now, by the prayer. Enter into it. It is for you. Pay the price and enter into prayer-rulership.

What of the foolish arguments of people who do not want to believe in the Lord Jesus? What of their unbelief? Are we able to come against such weapons of the wicked one? The biblical answer is yes. One hundred times yes. The Word of God says, *"For the weapons of our warfare are not worldly but have divine power to destroy strongholds. We destroy arguments and EVERY proud obstacle to the knowledge of God, and take every thought captive to obey Christ"* (2 Corinthians 10:4-5). Yes we have divine weapons. We are fighting a spiritual battle by prayer. We can destroy all arguments against the Lord and His Gospel. We are able to destroy EVERY proud obstacle (including the devil) to the knowledge of God. We are able to take EVERY thought of every human being captive to obey Christ. We can rule and conquer and bring every kind of person to obey Christ.

However, there is a price to pay in order to do this. The Bible says, *"Being ready to punish every disobedience WHEN YOUR OBEDIENCE IS COMPLETE"* (2 Corinthians 10:6). Only the completely obedient can unseat the devil completely. Can God find completely obedient servants? Will God find servants whose obedience is complete to use in this kind of warfare? Is your obedience complete? Will you allow Him to work mightily in you now to render your obedience to Him complete? What is the price? Pay it and conquer.

WHAT IF WE ARE SUDDENLY ATTACKED?

It is possible to be born again in a country where, due to the failure of the Church to put the devil in his right place, the devil's stronghold is thoroughly established. You may, on the other hand, be a pioneer in a place where Jesus has not yet been named and therefore the devil is on the offensive, or you may be suddenly and fiercely attacked by the wicked one. What are you to do? The prophet

Jeremiah has an answer for all in these kinds of situations and for
the Church in such situations. He says to the Lord, "You are my
hammer and weapon of war. With you I break nations to pieces;
with you I destroy kingdoms; with you I break in pieces man and
woman; with you I break in pieces until all becomes pieces - impotent pieces. The psalmist added his word of approval to such warfare. He said *"All nations surround me; in the name of the Lord I cut
them off! They surrounded me on every side; in the name of the Lord I
cut them off! They surrounded me like bees, they blazed like a fire of
thorns; in the name of the Lord I cut them off!"* (Psalm 118:10-12).
This is the way of victory. Such warfare wrecks the Enemy's kingdom. It destroys and sows confusion in that kingdom so much so
that the Enemy is able to turn and destroy itself.

Nehemiah's example

Nehemiah had a divine commission, but there were adversaries.
He tells the story himself. He says, *"When the enemies heard that it
was known that God had frustrated their plan, we all returned to the wall,
each to his work. From that day on, half of my servants worked on
construction and half held the spears, shields, bows, and coats of mail and
the leaders stood behind all the house of Judah who were building on the
wall. Those who carried burdens were laden in such a way that each with
one hand laboured on the work and with the other hand held his weapon.
And each of the builders had his sword girded at his side as he built. The
man who sounded the trumpet was beside me. And I said to the nobles and
to the officials and to the rest of the people, 'The work is great and widely
spread, and we are separated on the wall far from each other. In the place
where you hear the sound of the trumpet, rally to us here. Our God will
fight for us.' So we laboured at the work; and half of them held the spears
from the break of dawn till the stars came out. I also said to the people
at that time, 'Let every man and his servant pass the night within Jerusalem that they may be a guard for us by night and may labour by day.
So neither I nor my brethren nor my servants nor the men of the guard who*

followed me, none of us took off our clothes, each kept his weapon in his hand' "(Nehemiah 4:15-23).

There are many important lessons here. They were prepared both for building and for battle. One hand built and one hand held the weapon. All of them were involved without exception. They guarded as they built and they put up a guard for the night.

The time has come when the prayer warriors of God must not only pray, "Hallowed be Thy name, Thy Kingdom come and Thy will be done," wonderful as this is, but they must also pray down the Enemy kingdom and pray out his will. There must be mighty deliberate efforts in prayer not only to build the glorious Kingdom of the Lord but also to pull down the wicked kingdom of the devil. We are to direct part of our attention to praying and establishing the will of the Lord and the other part to purposely undoing the will of the wicked one. We are to find joy and satisfaction in the overthrow of Satan's will. Everything done to establish God's Kingdom will win His approval, and everything done to pull down the devil's kingdom will also win His approval. Ultimately, the two are interrelated, for we cannot fully establish God's Kingdom until we have brought down that of the Enemy. We cannot plunder the house until the strong man of the house has been bound. We must bind the devil.

Such a task can be carried out by individual believers only to a small extent. God has not given such a task merely to individuals. It is the task of the whole Church; and, in each locality, it is the task of the local church. Each member of the Church must be involved. In Nehemiah's day there were no exceptions. We cannot afford exceptions today. Again I say that it is the task of the whole Church to fight this kind of prayer battle with God against the devil.

The Church is put on a permanent guard against the wicked one. It is not enough to pray for two hours a week. It is not enough to pray one whole night a week. This is good. It should be encouraged, but it is not enough. Can you imagine a war in which one party fights a few hours some days and for the rest of the time they are doing other things and at night all sleep? Does it not become even more difficult to understand when it is clearly understood that the Enemy side is strong with multitudes of soldiers of all kinds?

We all know that the devil is most active at night. Being the Prince of Darkness he carries out some of his greatest exploits at night. What is the Church doing at night? Sleeping! What should she be doing? Some of her members should be watching and praying.

I have been thinking about these issues for some time now. I see only one thing that ought to and must be done. It is this: our local church in Yaoundé and other local churches ought to put up a twenty-four-hour watching with prayer. It should be well thought out, well prayed through, and practically implemented. At every minute of the night and the day, there should be people praying to the Lord on the one hand and praying down the wicked one on the other hand.

God will fight for us. God is fighting for us. May we fight wit Him. The Lord Jesus said: "My Father works, therefore I work." May we, too, say, "Our Lord is fighting for us, therefore we too fight with Him." Glory be to His name!

CHAPTER 4

The spiritual art of prayer :

GOD'S WILL AND WAITING

ON GOD

THE WILL OF GOD

KNOWING THE WILL OF GOD

Since prayer is the union of a believer's will with the will of God, it is imperative that a person should find out what God's will about a certain matter is, before he starts to pray. This is vital because God will only answer prayers that are prayed according to His will. Both the content and purpose of prayer must be according to the will of God.

God has promised to reveal His will to His praying children. He says, *"I will instruct you and teach you the way you should go; I will counsel you with my eye upon you"* (Psalms 32:8). *"He leads the humble in what is right, and teaches the humble his way"* (Psalms 25:8)- When a believer sincerely desires to know God's will about a certain matter, God will not keep that one in ignorance or suspense. He will reveal His will to him.

GOD'S WILL KNOWN BY PRAYING

The believer who wants to know God's will about a certain matter should bring that issue to the Lord. He should pray and say to the Lord, *"Make me to know Thy ways, O Lord; teach me Thy paths. Lead me in Thy truth, and teach me for Thou art the God of my salvation; for Thee I wait all the day long"* (Psalms 25:4-5). When he has thus prayed, he must wait before the Lord in prayer, and the Lord will make His will about that matter clear to him in his spirit. He can trust God to reveal His will.

However, to receive guidance from the Lord about a certain matter, the person seeking God's will must have a dealing with the Holy Spirit about that matter so that he has no selfish interests about the matter. It must be that the Holy Spirit has so worked out in his life about the matter that the person put his interests aside and just asks,

"Where are the interests of Jesus in this matter? I want to know the interest of Jesus and make them mine." At this point, with no selfish interests to cloud things, God's will is imparted at once. Sometimes it takes time for the Holy Spirit to bring us to the place where we are spiritually able to receive the revelation of God's will. This makes waiting in prayer important.

IDENTIFICATION WITH GOD'S WILL

When God's will has been received during prayer, the believer has to allow the Holy Spirit to work in his life so that he:

1. Loves God's will in a deep way, even if that will brought his cherished hopes to an end. Without this love for God's will, it will be difficult to enjoy doing it.

2. Identifies completely with God's will. He does not only love God's will, but he makes God's will his will. He unites God's will with his will so that there is just one will - God's will that incorporates the believer's will.

Having now only one will, which is God's perfect will, the believer can now engage in prayer so that this will should be established. Since God's will is good and perfect, the believer now engages in prayer to insist that God should bring that will to pass. He can then insist, cry, et cetera without ceasing, for under normal circumstances God does not change His will. Praying then from a God-sanctioned position, the believer can press on relentlessly, since that will must surely come to pass. He is prepared to insist day after day, month after month, and year after year with full assurance that the answer must come. For how can God fail to bring His will to pass? The Lord said, "*My counsel shall stand, and I will accomplish ALL My purpose*" (Isaiah 46:0). A true praying saint is one who will, night and day, cry to God, saying, "Father, let your will in this matter be fulfilled at any cost to me."

BURDEN FOR THE WILL OF GOD

It is not enough that the believer should be identified with God's will and want it to come to pass. He must ask and receive from the Lord a special burden to see the will of God accomplished. This burden will make the will of God weigh very heavily on his spirit, so much so that the only thing he will be able to do to be at ease, is to discharge that burden in unceasing prayer. Thus prayer would inwardly become an absolute necessity for the spirit to experience normalcy, for who could continue endlessly with an undischarged burden?

THE RIGHT MOTIVE FOR WANTING THE WILL OF GOD

There is the possibility that a person may be committed to the will of God because that will coincides with his will, because that will fits so much in the same direction with his own will such that following it will cause him no loss. It is possible that a person may love God's will and pray for its accomplishment because it will advance some secret motive, gratify something of the flesh in the person. If there are such wrong motives, it is obvious that such a person cannot fully satisfy God. His prayer will lack weight.

Before a person's prayer can satisfy God, the person praying must seek God's will for God's glory to be done. He must have no personal interests about the whole matter. If we pray in God´s will because it will help people to see how "spiritual" we are, we shall suffer absolute loss before God. Before a person prays rightly, he must himself be right; he must not only know the blood to deal away with sin, he must know the cross to deal away with self.

WAITING IN PRAYER

There are many reasons why waiting is important in prayer. The most important has to do with the preparation of the believer to receive the revelation of God's will, but there are other important aspects to it.

WAITING IN PREPARATION FOR TALKING TO GOD

My beloved father, Solomon Tanee Fomum, and I were intimate. The relationship transcended a loving father-son relationship. It grew into a very deep friendship, and I came to be perfectly free and transparent before my father. I could talk to him about anything that was on my mind. However intimate we were, I never lost respect of my father and never forgot the fact that he was my father and I his son. I never just rushed into his presence and started talking to him carelessly or disrespectfully. I never shouted at him. I always came before him with loving respect and waited before him quietly until he asked me or just let me know that I could speak. Even in the last years of his earthly life, when our relationship had matured and reached its apex and I had made some success in the acquisition of earthly honour, that respect remained and grew.

In the Lord Jesus, the Eternal God became our Father. Eternal holiness has accepted, by condescending love, to establish a loving Father-son relationship with us, who only have created holiness (In Christ). We will never be equal to God. We will never be equal to the Lord Jesus. The way in which some believers come into the presence of God, or carelessly address the Lord Jesus as their Brother, has never ceased to bother me. I consider it carnal rudeness.

The Bible says, *"Guard your steps when you go to the house of God; to draw near to listen is better than to offer the sacrifice of fools; for they do not know that they are doing evil. BE NOT RASH WITH YOUR MOUTH, NOR LET YOUR HEART BE HASTY TO UTTER A*

WORD BEFORE GOD, for God is in heaven and you upon earth; therefore let your words be few. For a dream comes with much business, AND A FOOL'S VOICE WITH MANY WORDS" (Ecclesiastes 5:1 -3).

So when we come before the Lord, le us come respectfully. Let us allow some time for the Holy Spirit to create in us the quiet spirit that is indispensable to prayer. Let us allow Him to create in us a holy awareness of God's presence. Let us allow Him to cut off the noise and thoughts of the world around us; then we can enter into His presence.

This basic preparation is necessary, also, because it helps us to concentrate in prayer. Many problems with wandering thoughts in prayer can be traced to this lack of preparation to enter into His presence. I personally find that the reading of a few verses of scripture or the quiet singing of a hymn of praise calms my being down and makes me ready to enter into His holy presence. Of course, in times of emergency this may not be possible or necessary, but all of prayer is not emergency – it is fellowship.

If, after some time before the Lord, there is no calmness in the inner man, we should go ahead and just ask the Lord to create a spiritual calm. As we ask Him, the Holy Spirit may show us that the lack of calmness is owing to some unconfessed sin or a broken relationship with someone which needs to be confessed or put right before we can pray. If He has graciously shown us that, then we have only one way open to us - to obey.

WAITING TO KNOW GOD'S WILL

Before a person begins to wait before the Lord, he should settle it in his mind that he will not act until God has made His will clear. For to come before the Lord and ask Him to reveal His will to you and, after asking, to go away without hearing from the Lord and carrying our some action is tragic foolishness. All, therefore, who wait must be determined to suspend all action until the Lord has made His will clear. God will reveal His will to such people. Waiting will benefit such people. The others who are prepared to ask and not wait for answers should not bother to start the exercise at all. Waiting stems from the knowledge that God is committed to reveal His will to those who ask Him and that even if it takes long for the revelation to come to me, it will nevertheless come.

Waiting is also a confession of ignorance both of ourselves and of God. As we have said earlier, the Holy Spirit needs to bring us to a place where we are prepared to go in any direction He leads, having no personal selfish ambition about it. I find my own heart so deceptive that, even when I think that I have no personal interests in a matter, I yet want to wait before the Lord for His searchlight, lest I be self-deceived. I have daily to confess not only my ignorance of God and His ways but also my profound ignorance of myself. This makes waiting a basic must.

The Bible says, *"Our soul waits for the Lord; He is our help and shield"* (Psalms 33:20). *"For God alone my soul waits in silence; from Him comes my salvation"* (Psalms 62:1). *"For God alone my soul waits in silence, for my hope is from Him"* (Psalms 62:5). *"I wait for the Lord, my soul waits, and in His word I hope; my soul waits for the Lord more than watchmen for the morning"* (Psalms 130:5-6). *"It will be said on that day, lo, this is our God; we have waited for Him; let us be glad and rejoice in His salvation"* (Isaiah 25:9). *"O Lord, be gracious to us; we wait for Thee. Be our arm every morning, our salvation in the time of trouble"* (Isaiah 33:2).

God will impart His will by revelation to the waiting heart. He will not allow those who wait on Him to be put to shame. He will not allow them to be mistaken. He will draw near to them. He will be their sure help.

WAITING TO KNOW THE DIRECTION IN WHICH TO PRAY

Even when God's will has been revealed to us, we still need to wait on the Lord in order to know how to pray that will to accomplishment. For example, we may receive from the Lord the fact that He wants a particular part of the country reached by us with the Gospel. That is good. However, the questions then arise, "How are we to pray this through to realization? Do we just start praying for conversions there?" I do not think so. We must first realize the role of the Holy Spirit in that particular aspect of God's will. He is the director of God's Missionary Enterprise. He is also the director of deep prayer. Having known God's will, we must still wait on the Holy Spirit in order to know where to begin in prayer. He will lead us maybe to pray first that the Lord will lay the burden for those people on some hearts, so that they begin to pray about it day and night, or He may led us to pray for young Spirit-filled men who will take the Gospel there, or just another aspect. One thing is certain. He will lead those who wait on Him and He will pray side by side with such waiting, praying people. And what a blessing

WAITING FOR RENEWED STRENGTH IN PRAYER

Even when we are praying under the special guidance of the Holy Comforter, we sometimes get tired, or the burden may become so heavy that it comes very close to crushing us. At such moments, we need to wait on the Lord for renewed strength in prayer. We are commanded by the Lord to so wait. *"Wait for the Lord; be of good courage, and He shall strengthen thine heart. Wait, I say, on the Lord"* (Psalms 27:14AV). The command is the Lord's, and those who obey it find blessing in it. The Bible says, *"He gives power to the faint, and to him who has no might he increases strength. Even youths shall faint, and be weary and young men shall fall exhausted; but they who wait for the Lord shall renew their strength, they shall mount up with wings like eagles, they shall run and not be weary, they shall walk and not faint"* (Isaiah 40:29-31). Does this explain why some people can engage in mighty spiritual conflict for hours upon hours, yet seem not to lose their strength, while others are completely exhausted and crushed after just a few minutes of praying?

WAITING AND THE NEEDS OF GOD

I write it very humbly but very confidently that God has "needs," personal needs which He has decided in His sovereignty to have and which can be revealed only to a few of His closest friends. These closest friends of God are those who love Him supremely and love only Him. This love will drive them to spend hours, days, and even years before Him, waiting that He may reveal His needs to them. Such saints will consider one second spent at meeting the personal "needs" of Deity of greater worth than billions of years spent in serving the sons of men.

If you are one of those supreme lovers of God, I invite you to habitually draw apart to wait on Him. He will not reveal His needs to you the first time that you wait on Him. He will call you to further and longer periods of waiting on Him, and at the height of that waiting and longing after Him, He will reveal His "needs" to you. After that your spiritual service will never, I repeat, "never" be the same.

I wonder whether you feel in your heart that you dare to attempt an entry into such a walk with God. It is wonderful, but there are three basic requirements, all of them out of tune with the desires of the flesh: There is, first of all, utter purity. God will require of you a hatred for sin which He does not seem to demand from other believers. He will also demand from you a degree of consecration to His will and to His purposes that will leave room for nothing of your own interests. Secondly, waiting on God is lonely business. You will, in a way, withdraw from the world around you and be shut up in God's world. Yet at the very beginning of your waiting, God will seem to withdraw even His very presence, which you so badly need. As it were, you will be lonely, cut off from man and "cut off" from God for a "season". Are you prepared for that? The Lord of glory, Jesus Christ, suffered this in Gethsemane. He suffered the knowledge that on the cross the Father would forsake Him, and He found this separation from the Father (the cup) so undesirable that He wanted it to be taken away. You, too, will know that in some way you may complete that which is lacking in the suffering of Christ.

Thirdly, God will reveal things to you during your time of waiting on Him that He will not allow you to share with anyone else. If He reveals to you His personal need, it will often be that He will not want you to share it with anyone else. He may give you a yoke, a burden to bear for Him which would be easier to bear if you told someone else, but which He will not allow you to share. He may lead you to take a pathway that will cause you to be misunderstood by many whom you love, a pathway along which, were you to explain, would cause you to be understood, appreciated, and even admired; but at His demand, you will keep silent and be despised for it and even thought to have backslidden. Are you prepared to bear burdens, God's burdens, unaided, misunderstood by man? If you are, tell God you are prepared. He will weigh your heart to see if your heart and your words are in the same direction. If they are, He will take you into this special confidence and blessed are you!

THE WAITING GOD FOR A WAITING PEOPLE

The Bible says, "*Therefore the Lord waits to be gracious to you, therefore He exalts Himself to show mercy to you. For the Lord is a God of justice; blessed are those who wait for Him*" (Isaiah 30:18). The great Almighty is prepared to wait for us that He may be gracious to us. How wonderful! He in return wants people who wait upon Him. When a waiting God and a waiting people meet, very great things take place. May we, you and I, be that people. We shall surely receive mercy from His hand. Glory be to His name!

A BEGINNER IN THE SCHOOL OF WAITING

The "School of Waiting" is one of the important academies in the life of prayer. The subject there are not easily mastered and theoretical knowledge is of very little help. I want to encourage you, nevertheless, to begin. Even if you do not know what to do, tell the Lord Almighty that you want to learn how to wait before Him and that you actually want to grow as a waiting, praying saint. He will answer you quickly, but He will not just impart to you an overwhelming capacity to wait before the Lord; for you will not be able to use it. He will teach you a little at a time. Sometimes your progress will seem so little that you will wonder if you are learning at all. Nevertheless, do not give up. You are in the School. He is your Teacher. He will never fail you. He has taught many students who have made progress. He will not allow you to be the exception. Wait on Him, as He teaches you. Trust Him to teach you; slowly but certainly, step after step, you will make progress in this "Academy" with God. Dearest friend, I pray for you as you begin. God bless you. God enable you.

CHAPTER 5

The spiritual art of prayer :

THE BELIEVER'S PERSONAL NEEDS

THE COMMITMENT OF GOD

It is now obvious that prayer only satisfies the heart of God if it is prayed in the will of God and for the glory of God. All other motives for prayer are not considered by the Lord who answers prayer.

An important question then arises: Can God fail to answer prayer that is in His perfect will? The unchanging answer is no! Absolutely no! The Lord has committed Himself to answer prayer.

HEAVEN GOVERNED BY EARTH

The Lord Jesus said, *"Verily I say unto you, what things so ever ye shall bind on earth SHALL BE, having been bound in heaven, and whatever things ye loose on earth shall be, having been loosed in heaven"* (Matthew 18:18). This is a very far-reaching commitment! It means that there is absolutely no possibility that we can bind on earth in accordance with the will of God for the sole glory of God and that binding fails to be accomplished. If there were to be such failure, the Word of God would be proved untrue, God would be shown to be a liar and the principle that holds the whole universe would collapse. God even went beyond that. He said that whatever was loosed on earth would be loosed in heaven. He did not suggest, even in the slightest way, that there was any possibility, however small, that earth's loosing would pass in vain. We can be absolutely sure that provided we satisfy God's conditions ALL that we bind or loose on earth SHALL BE. Let all who read this bear in mind that the Word of God says, "Whatever" That includes everything except nothing.

I am thoroughly amazed by that commitment by God. He has, in His sovereignty, decided that the dictates of heaven will wait for earth's corresponding action, and that unless that action by earth is forthcoming, heaven will temporarily remain inactive. May the

Church take care not to allow such a commitment to go in vain. When earth (the Church) delays to take action, heaven waits!!

THE POWER OF THE CHURCH

The Lord Jesus further said, "*Again I say to you, if two of you agree on earth about ANYTHING they ask, it will be done for them by my Father in heaven. For where two or three are gathered in my name, there I am in the midst of them*" (Matthew 18:19-20). Here is a further commitment on the Lord's part. It is a commitment to people who are gathered in the name of the Lord. It is not a commitment to just any gathering of individuals. The people who are concerned here are people who are not meeting after the will of man or the will of the flesh, but who are gathered, brought together by the Lord. This is the Church; for the Church is not just the company of any believers assembling according to their whims or traditions or doctrines. The Church is a band of Christ-lovers brought together by the Holy Spirit. He gathers them together and dwells in their midst. He is so present that when they ask, He is involved in the asking. Since He gave them origin, He also initiates all their asking, which then all is according to the Father's will. Thus we see why God can commit Himself so deeply. He gathers them. He causes them to agree. He dwells fully in their midst. He reveals to them the will of the Father. He causes them to transform that will into prayer requests, and together with them those requests are presented to the Father. The Father does exactly as they have asked. So we see that that is true prayer. The requests originated in the will of God. God was their originator. He committed His thoughts through Christ to the Church. The Church, in the power of the Holy Spirit, presents the will of God to Him as requests, and God unfailingly answers. He can't do otherwise.

The Power of the Individual Believer

In one verse after another in the Word, God has committed Himself to individual believers that He will answer all their prayers that originate in Him and end in Him. The Lord Jesus said, "*Whatever you ask in my name, I will do it that the Father may be glorified in the Son*" (John 14:13). "*If you ask anything in my name, I will do it*" (John 14:14). "*You did not choose me but I choose you and appointed you that you should go and bear fruit and that your fruit should abide, so that whatever you ask the Father in my name He will give you*" (John 15:16). "*Hitherto you have asked nothing in my name; ask and it will be given to you*" (Matthew 7:7). "*Everyone who asks receives*" (Matthew 7:8). "*And whatever you ask in prayer, you will receive if you have faith*" (Matthew 21:22). "*Ask and it will be given to you*" (Luke 11:9). "*Whatever you ask in prayer, believe that you received it and it shall be yours*" (Mark 11:24). "*The desire of the righteous shall be granted*" (Proverbs 10:24).

I am personally surprised by the frequency of the word "ask". God wants people to ask. Asking shows that we have confidence in Him. Asking also portrays humility. If a person does not ask, he is either too foolish or too proud or both. Many people, instead of asking, just wish. But the Bible does not say "wish". It says "ask". Others, instead of asking, hope. But the Bible does not say "hope". It says "ask". Some, instead of asking, plan to ask, but never get down to asking; and so they never receive. May God bring all His children to the point where they ask and ask and ask. There is no way out.

I am also surprised by the frequency of the words "whatever" and "anything." This means that there is no limit to what we can ask in the will of God. God is fabulously and immensely rich. He is richer than we shall ever know, be it in time or eternity. When we begin to ask in His will and receive great things from Him, we shall only be scratching the surface of a limitless mine. Do you think that the 'whatever' and 'anything' of God's will are few or limited?

I say to you, no! No!! This is a mine to be explored. God has so much to give and He has such wonderful things to give that His one surprise, nay, disappointment, is that there are too few who ask, and these few who ask are afraid to ask much. The Word of God says, *"What no eye has seen, nor ear heard, nor the heart of man conceived, what God has prepared for those who love Him"* (1 Corinthians 2:9). God has these wonderful things in store. He has prepared them for us – things never before seen nor heard of. They are there waiting to be received upon asking. These things are not just for the future, they are for the here and now, for He surely wants to bless us very richly. The Bible says, *"For the eyes of the Lord run to and fro throughout the whole earth, to show His might in behalf of those whose heart is blameless toward Him"* (2 Chronicles 16:9).

I am also surprise by the words "It will be given to you"; "He will give you," et cetera. God means just that. Some times it sounds too good to be believed, but that is it. God means it. Do you believe it?

THE BELIEVER'S PERSONAL NEEDS

Sometimes we seem to say, "Well, if I pray about souls, God will hear me; but what of my personal needs? What of my needs of food, clothing, journeying mercies, education, health, marriage, et cetera? Does God care? Will He answer?" Let me state very clearly that God is involved with the total man. He is concerned for the needs of the spirit, soul, and body. Hezekiah prayed for more years and had them. Hannah prayed for a son and had one. Ezra prayed for journeying mercies and they were granted to him. The Lord taught us to pray and ask for food. He is a very practical God. He is totally involved. We must bring all our needs and desires to Him. His word says, *"The desires of the righteous shall be granted"* (Proverbs 10:24). Some people are too "spiritual" to be involved with the issues of daily life! The Lord Jesus was involved; He fed the hungry, wept with the mourners, et cetera.

The measure of a man's maturity with God is the extent to which he is prepared to allow God to permeate every area of his life. If he cannot pray or does not pray about some area(s) of his life, his Christianity must be considered sublevel. The truly spiritual person will ask God for kingdoms: for the Lord said, "*Ask of me, and I will make the nations your heritage and the ends of the earth you possession*" (Psalms 2:8), and he will pray, saying. "*Lord, give me today the bread that I need for breakfast tomorrow morning." This is genuine spirituality. "Thou hast given him his heart's desire, and hast not withheld the request of his lips*" (Psalms 21:2). "*Delight thyself in the Lord and He shall give thee the desire of thine heart*" (Psalms 37:4). "*No good thing does He withhold from those who walk uprightly*" (Psalms 84:11). "*In thy strength the king rejoices. O Lord; and in thy help how greatly he exults! Thou hast given him his heart's desire, and hast not withheld the request of his lips. For Thou dost meet him with goodly blessings; Thou gavest it to him, length of days for ever and ever. His glory is great through thy help; splendour and majesty Thou dost bestow upon him. Yes, Thou dost make him most blessed for ever; Thou dost make him glad with the joy of Thy presence*" (Psalms 21:1-6).

The Bible abounds with examples of men and women who asked in prayer and got their personal needs. Whatever these were, they were met by the Lord. We shall briefly look at some of these.

FOR CONVICTION OF SIN

"*Make me know my transgression and my sin*" (Job 13:23). "*Search me, O God and know my heart! Try me and know my thoughts! And see if there be any wicked way in me, and lead me in the way everlasting*" (Psalms 139:23-24). "*Prove me, O Lord and try me; test my heart and my mind*" (Psalms 26:2). We need to pray this prayer at the deepest personal level and to wait before God to be shown what He sees us to be, for our hearts are terribly deceitful. Unless sin is dealt with at the deepest level, it will be impossible to prevail in prayer. Is this not our greatest personal need ?

FOR CLEANSING AND PARDON OF SIN

"For Thy name's sake, O Lord, pardon my guilt, for it is great" (Psalms 25:11). *"Consider my affliction and my trouble, and forgive all my sins"* (Psalms 25:18).*"Deliver me from all my transgressions"* (Psalms 39:8). *"Have mercy on me, O God, according to Thy steadfast love; according to Thy abundant mercy blot out my transgressions. Wash me thoroughly from my iniquity, and cleanse me from my sins"* (Psalms 51:1-2). *"Purge me with hyssop, and I shall be clean. Wash me, and I shall be whiter than snow"* (Psalms 51:7). These are basic, yet far-reaching prayers. I who write this have prayed them time and again, for my own sin is great. These are, however, very personal matters that take place in the intimacy of the inner man. These are deep transactions with God. The superficial know nothing about them.

FOR KNOWLEDGE OF DIVINE THINGS

"Moses said to the Lord, see Thou sayest to me, bring up this people, but Thou hast not let me know whom Thou wilt send with me. Yet Thou hast said, I know you by name, and you have also found favour in my sight. Now therefore, I pray Thee, if I have found favour in Thy sight, show me now Thy ways, that I may know Thee and find favour in Thy sight" (Exodus 33:12-13). *"Make me know Thy ways, O Lord; teach me Thy path, lead me in Thy truth and teach me"* (Psalms 25:4-5). *"Teach me to do Thy will, for Thou art my God! Let Thy good spirit lead me on a level path"* (Psalms 143:10). If we are to make progress in the School of Prayer, we must know the Lord to whom we pray in a deeper way and know His ways in a more intimate and clearer way. There is no substitute for this.

PERSONAL REVIVAL

Many people go on with the Lord and somewhere along the line they lose their personal touch with the Lord and sink into routine activity. Such need revival. They must pray for it. It is a personal need. *"My soul cleaves to the dust; revive me according to Thy Word"* (Psalms 119:25). *"Turn my eyes from looking at vanities; and give me life in Thy ways"* (Psalms 119:37). *"Behold, I long for Thy precepts; in Thy righteousness give me life"* (Psalms 11:40) *"Restore us again, O God of our salvation, and put away Thy indignation toward us! Wilt Thou be angry with us for ever? Wilt Thou prolong Thy anger to all generations? Wilt Thou not revive us again, that Thy people may rejoice in Thee? Show us Thy steadfast love, and grant us Thy salvation"* (Psalms 85:4-7).

HELP IN TROUBLE

"But Thou, O Lord, be not far off! O Thou my help, hasten to my aid" (Psalms 22:19). "Incline Thy ear, O Lord, and answer me, for I am poor and needy" (Psalms 86:1). *"Make hast to answer me O Lord! My spirit fails! Hide not Thy face from me, lest I be like those who go down to the pit"* (Psalms 143:7).

FOR HEALING FROM SICKNESS CAUSED BY SIN

"O Lord, rebuke me not in Thy anger, nor chasten me in Thy wrath. Be gracious to me, O Lord, for I am languishing, O Lord, heal me, for my bones are troubled. My soul also is sorely troubled. But Thou, O Lord how long ?" (Psalms 6:1-3) *"O Lord, rebuke me not in Thy anger nor chasten me in Thy wrath! For Thy arrows have sunk into me, and Thy hand has come down on me. There is no soundness in my flesh because of Thy indignation; there is no health in my bones because of my sin"* (Psalms 38:1–3).

FOR SUCCESS IN BUSINESS (EXAMINATIONS, ET CETERA)

"Jabez called on the God of Israel, saying, 'Oh that Thou wouldst bless me and enlarge my border, and Thy Hand might be with me, and that

Thou wouldst keep me from harm so that it might not hurt me!" And God granted what he asked" (1 Chronicles 4:10). *"Let Thy work be manifest to Thy servants, and Thy glorious power to their children. Let the favour of the Lord our God be upon us, and establish Thou the work of our hands upon us, yes, the work of our hands establish Thou it"* (Psalms 20:16-17). *"Save us, we beseech Thee, O Lord! O Lord! We beseech Thee, give us success!"* (Psalms 118:25). *"O Lord, let Thy ear be attentive to the prayer of thy servant, and to the prayer of Thy servants who delight to fear Thy name; and give success to Thy servant today, and grant him mercy in the sight of this man"* (Nehemiah 1:11). *"And the king granted me what I asked for the good hand of my God was upon me"* (Nehemiah 2:8).

FAVOUR IN OLD AGE

"Do not cast me off in the time of old age; forsake me not when my strength is spent" (Psalms 71:9). *"O God, from my youth Thou hast taught me, and I still proclaim Thy wondrous deeds. So even to old age and gray hairs, O God, do not forsake me, till I proclaim Thy might to all generation to come"* (Psalms 71:17-18).

We should get right with God and then we can ask Him anything. One young woman asked me if she could ask God to touch her hair so that it might grow longer. I replied that God meant her hair to be for His glory, so he should ask the Lord to lengthen her hair. She did and God answered. Another asked God that she might look more attractive. The Lord answered by causing the pimples that marred her looks to disappear, and she really looks attractive now. People have asked for increased intelligence and received a greater capacity for understanding the sciences and the arts than was theirs naturally. The list is inexhaustible. When you pray, you are coming before the King. Ask for great things but also ask anything that causes you concern. Nothing is too small for Him to attend to. Nothing is too big for Him to supply. He is all in all. Glory be to His Holy Name !

THE NAME OF JESUS

The Lord Jesus did not teach us to pray to Himself. He taught that prayer was to be addressed to God the Father in His (Jesus) name. Let us stop praying to the Lord Jesus but pray to God the Father in the name of Jesus. Jesus said, *"If you ask anything in my name, I will do it."* So we ask the Father in the name of Jesus, and the Father will then ask Jesus to do the things we want. What are the implications of the name of Jesus? Why has the Father committed Himself to answering prayer that is prayed in the Son's name? I immediately think of the following reasons:

1.   **The name of Jesus talks of access, merit**. You can approach God because Jesus has taken away the barrier of sin. You come into the presence of God, not because of personal worth, but because Jesus is altogether worthy. You may be unworthy, but you come on the basis of one who is altogether worthy. Because of Christ, you should come with boldness. Do not let the devil tell you that you are not worthy. Come. Jesus says, "You are worthy."

2.   **The name of Jesus talks of authority**. This is, first of all, authority before God. Jesus is the exalted Son of God. God cannot refuse any request of the Son. So He will not refuse a request made in the name of the Son. To ask in the name of Jesus means that the prayer is made on grounds that the Father cannot refuse. The name of Jesus also signifies authority before the wicked one. Jesus defeated him. He knows that before Jesus he has no authority whatsoever. To ask in the name of Jesus is to ask on grounds which make satanic resistance null and void. The devil knows that, and he fears and trembles!

3.   **'In the name of Jesus' means that the petition is such as Jesus would have made if He had been in our situa-**

tion. If we are to ask in the name of Jesus, we must ask ourselves, "If Christ were in my situation, would He make this request to the Father?" We cannot use His name to back up things with which He would not at all be identified. It will just not work. His name and His person are one; and where His person would refuse to be involved, His name will not be effective. If it is used, it will just be empty words.

4. **"In the name of Jesus" means that that prayer is made for the glory of God, for the building of the Church, and for the overthrow of Satan.**

BELIEVING IS SEEING : ASSURANCE IN PRAYER

BELIEVING AND RECEIVING

In the natural realm it is generally said, "Seeing is believing." When you see, then you believe. This, however, is not the case in the spiritual dimension. The Lord Jesus persistently put believing before seeing. He said, *"If you can! All things are possible to him who believes"* (Mark 9:23). *"Have you believed because you have seen me? Blessed are those who have not seen and yet believe"* (John 20:29).

The apostle said, *"And this is the confidence which we have in Him, that if we ask anything according to His will, He hears us. And if we know that He hears us in whatever we ask, we KNOW that we have obtained the request made of Him"* (1 John 5:14-15). We can write out the following five stages in prayer:

1. Confidence in the Lord. This confidence is basic. It is absolutely essential to prayer. The Bible says, *"And without faith it is impossible to please Him. For whoever would draw near to God must believe that He exists and that He rewards those who*

seek Him" (Hebrews 11:6). To pray without confidence in the Lord is a big waste of time, and, worse than that, it is mocking God.

2. Ask (according to His will).
3. Know that God hears. Sometimes we shout as if God were dead.
4. Know that because He hears us in whatever we ask, we have obtained (before seeing) the request made of Him.
5. See what we received.

In the Gospel of Mark, the same principle is presented this way, "*Have faith in God. Truly, I say to you, whoever says to this mountain, 'Be taken up and cast into the sea,' and does not doubt in his heart, but believes that what he says will come to pass, it will be done for him. Therefore I tell you, whatever you ask in prayer, believe that you have received it and it will be yours*" (Mark 11:22-24). Here again we have:

1. **Confidence in God (have faith in God).**
2. **Ask.**
3. **Believe**
4. **Receive before seeing.**
5. **See what you received.**

So, the praying believer receives by faith what he has asked of the Lord before he has had any physical evidence of the answer, and then afterwards sees by sight what be received without "sight." To put in the other words, the person sees by spiritual sight, receives by spiritual sight, and then sees by physical sight that which he already saw and received by spiritual sight.

SPIRITUAL SIGHT AND IMPORTUNITY

The problem often arises in many hearts and they question in these ways, "How am I to reconcile the call to ask and keep asking until I receive with this asking and receiving before seeing? How do I know that I have received by faith before I have seen so that I can stop asking? Is there no danger that I may stop asking that which has already been given and therefore betray doubt?"

The answer lies in the witness of the Holy Spirit to the spirit of the praying person. Since prayer is fundamentally communication from God through the Holy Spirit to the spirit of man and back from the spirit of man through the Holy Spirit to God, the one who walks close to the Lord and has a liberated spirit will know in his spirit that the answer has come, and he should stop praying. This inner, personal relationship between the believer's spirit and the Holy Spirit is indispensable for deep praying.

In this relationship between the Holy Spirit and the believer's spirit, a person will "know" whether to ask a thing once or twice or a thousand times. He will not look at the visible answer to know when to stop praying. He will receive from the Holy Spirit the revelation knowledge that the prayer has been answered, and he need not ask any more.

All this makes vital fellowship with the Lord indispensable to prayer, for only those who walk closely to Him will grow in this school of revelation knowledge.

THE WORD OF GOD

The Lord has made many promises in His Word. These promises are to be claimed in prayer and experienced by the believer. The Word of God is infallible. The psalmist said, "*For ever, O Lord Thy Word is firmly fixed in the heavens*" (Psalms 119:87). The apostle Peter said, "*The Word of the Lord abides of ever*" (1 Peter 1:25). The

Lord Himself said, *"Heaven and earth will pass away, but my words will not pass away"* (Matthew 24:35). If the Word is so infallible and so unchanging, how is it that some believers claim promises made in the Word and fail to see their claims fulfilled?

The first thing to be said here is that the fault cannot be with God and His Word. He and His word are thoroughly faultless. The problem must be with the believer. What we have in the Bible are the general promises of God to anyone. Who is anyone ? Who is whosoever? Anyone in the Bible sense is the one who fulfils God's requirements. The promises are for people who are prepared to walk close to God, know God, and ask in the same spirit with Him who has promised to answer. If someone who is out of tune with God were to claim a promise simply because the Bible says so, it would be necessary that his claim goes in vain or else God would become the promoter of unrighteousness.

The written Word of God must become the living Word of God applied to our hearts by the Holy Spirit. Faced with a given situation like, say, a sick and dying man, I need to hear the Lord saying to me, "I promised that those who believe in me would lay hands on the sick and they would recover. The person before you is one such person. I am going to heal him as you go ahead and lay hands upon him in my name." This is the personal Word from the Lord based upon the written infallible Word. No one can follow in this way and go wrong. If, on the other hand, we live at random and go laying hands on people for healing at random, we will find that often the promises in the Word do not work. How many people have laid hands on the sick in the name of the Lord Jesus and found that nothing happened? We read of great healing evangelists, but let us look at the facts: A man prays for a thousand sick people. Four are healed and all the rest are untouched. What happened? It must mean that only the four were ordained by the Lord to be touched and healed. Had the evangelist waited for the personal revelation from the Lord, he would have been led to lay hands only on the four. The

Holy Spirit must apply the unchanging promises of God's word to our hearts so that they become God's promises and God's special commitment to us as individuals, and then we can move ahead in full assurance that He will do what He has promised.

This revelation knowledge will enhance the reality of the Word experienced by the believer. It will enable prayer to be what God meant it to be: an intimate relationship between Him and His children. May the Lord lead us to that kind of knowledge.

CHAPTER 6

The spiritual art of prayer :

THE LIMITATIONS OF GOD

GOD'S HAND SHORTENED

The bible says, *"Behold, the Lord's hand is not shortened that it cannot save, or His ear dull, that it cannot hear; but your iniquities have made a separation between you and your God, and your sins have hid His face from you so that He does not hear"* (Isaiah 59:1,2). God's hand will never be shortened! God will never change position because people prefer to sin. One thing, however, is obvious: The sin of a believer will cause a separation between him and God and hide God's face from the believer. This means that the prayer of such a person will not be heard.

BOUNCING PRAYER

Prayer that comes from unrighteous hearts will bounce on the unrighteousness and return to the one who prayed from such a condition. The prayer of the unrighteous will not be heard by the Lord and will not be answered. The Bible says, *"Then the Ammorites who lived in that hill country came out against you and chased you as bees do and beat you down in Seir as far as Hormah. And you returned and wept before the Lord; but the Lord did no hearken to you voice or give ear to you"* (Deuteronomy 1:44-45). Moses prayed after he had sinned and the prayer was not answered. He put it this way, himself, *"And I besought the Lord at that time saying, 'O Lord God, Thou hast only begun to show Thy servant Thy greatness and Thy mighty hand; for what God is there in heaven or on earth who can do such works and mighty acts as Thine? Let me go over, I pray, and see the good land beyond the Jordan, that goodly hill country, and Lebanon'"* (Deuteronomy 3:23-25). It was a good prayer, but Moses was now out of favor. He had sinned and so he continued the narrative, *"But God the Lord was angry with me on you account, and would not hearken to me: and the Lord said to me, 'Let it suffice you; speak no more to me of this matter'"* (Deuteronomy 3:26). *"They looked, but there was none to save; they cried to the Lord but He did not answer them"* (2 Samuel 22:42). *"For what is the hope of the godless when God cuts him off, when God takes away his cry, when trouble comes upon him?"* (Job 27:8,9). The obvious answer is No. God will not hear his cry! *"They cried for help, but there was none to save, they cried to the Lord, but He did not answer them"* (Psalms 18:41). Proverb says, *"Because I have called and you refused to listen I have stretched out my hand and no one has heeded, and you have ignored all my counsel and would have none of my reproof, I also will laugh at your calamity; I will mock when panic strikes you, when panic strikes you like a storm, and your calamity comes like a whirlwind, when distress and anguish come upon you. Then they will call upon me, but I will not answer, they will seek me diligently but will not find me"* (Proverbs 1:24-28). *"Again the Lord said to me. 'There is revolt among the men of Judah and the inhabitants of Jerusalem. They have turned back to the iniquities of their forefathers, who refused to hear my words, they have gone after other gods to serve them; the house of Israel and the house of Judah have broken my covenant which I made with their fathers. Therefore, thus says the Lord, behold, I am bringing evil upon them which they cannot escape; though they cry to me I will not listen to them'"* (Jeremiah 11:9-11). *"Their deeds do not permit them to return to their God. For the spirit of harlotry is within them, and they know not the Lord... With their flocks and herds they shall go seek the Lord, but they will not find Him: He has withdrawn from them"* (Hosea 5:4-6). *"Then they will cry to the Lord, but He will not answer them. He will hide His face from them at that time, because they have made their deeds evil"* (Micah 3:4). *"They made their hearts like adamant lest they should hear the law and the words which the Lord of hosts had sent by His Spirit through the former prophets. Therefore great wrath came from the Lord of hosts. 'As I called, and they would not hear, so they called, and I would not hear,' says the Lord of hosts"* (Zechariah 7:12-13).

WORLDLINESS

"You ask and do not receive because you ask wrongly, to spend it on your passions. Unfaithful creatures! Do you not know that friendship with the world is enmity with God? Therefore whoever wishes to be a friend of the world makes himself an enemy of God" (James 4:3-4). To ask God things so that we can be like the people of the world, compare well with them, win their favours, et cetera, is to court the disfavor of God. Friendship is the product of much cultivation. We can cultivate the friendship of God or the friendship of the world.

All cultivation begins in the heart, with desire. If there is just the slightest desire to be worldly, we already lose favour with God and lose our grounds for having our prayers answered. If that is the case, we must put things right before we can pray. James has the prescription: *"Submit yourselves therefore to God. Resist the devil and he will flee from you. Draw near to God and He will draw near to you. Cleanse your hands, you sinners, and purify your hearts, you men of double mind. Be wretched and mourn and weep. Let your laughter be turned to mourning and your joy to dejection. Humble yourselves before the Lord and He will exalt you"* (James 4:7-10). The cure to worldliness is not in superficial external acts like getting rid of some things. The cure lies in purified hearts. It must be a deep work. This work can only be carried out by the Holy Spirit in those hearts that see worldliness as a most dangerous sin and are prepared to pay the price for the radical surgery which is necessary to get rid of it.

MERCILESSNESS

The Bible says, *"He who closes his ear to the cry of the poor will himself cry out and not be heard"* (Proverbs 21:13). *"Is such the fast that I choose, a day for a man to humble himself? Is it to bow down his dead like a rush, and to spread sackcloth and ashes under him? Will you call this a fast and a day acceptable to the Lord? Is not this the fast that I choose: to loose the bonds of wickedness, to undo the thongs of the yoke, to let the oppressed go free, and to break every yoke? Is it not to share your bread with the hungry, and bring the homeless poor into your house; when you see the naked, to cover him, and not to hide yourself from your own flesh? Then shall your light break forth like the dawn, and your healing shall spring up speedily; your righteousness shall go before you, the glory of the Lord shall be your rear guard. THEN YOU SHALL CALL AND THE LORD WILL ANSWER; YOU SHALL CRY, AND HE WILL SAY, HERE I AM"* (Isaiah 58:5-9).

The point is this: If we are unconcerned about the needs of others, if we will not hear their cry, if we refuse to be used by God to meet their needs, then God will, in turn, recompense us accordingly. It is only fair play!

The Lord continues to make this point sharply. He says, *"For if you forgive men their trespasses, your heavenly Father will also forgive you; but if you do not forgive men their trespasses, neither will your Father forgive your trespasses"* (Matthew 6:14-15). *"Therefore I tell you, whatever you ask in prayer, believe that you have received it, and it will be yours. And whenever you stand praying, forgive, if you have anything against anyone; so that your Father also who is in heaven may forgive you your trespasses"* (Mark 11:24-25).

The logic is this: God will only hear the prayers of people who are purified. An unforgiving spirit immediately cuts God off. Much prayer will not change the situation, since the prayers will not be heard. Only one thing will do: Forgive the offending party. Since prayer is a sort of sacrifice (it is sometimes the sacrifice of praise), the Bible says, *"So if you are offering you gift at the altar, and there remember that your brother has something against you, leave your gift there before the altar and go; first be reconciled to your brother, then come and offer your gift"* (Matthew 5:23-24).

PRAYER A BURDEN TO GOD

The Bible says, "*If one turns away from hearing the law, even his prayer is an abomination*" (Proverbs 28:9). When a person abides in sin and prays as if everything were all right, his prayer is an abomination to God. To a sin-ridden Israel God said: "*When you come to appear before me who requires of you this trampling of my courts? Bring no more vain offerings; incense is an abomination to me. New moon and sabbath and the calling of assemblies; I cannot endure iniquity and solemn assembly. Your new moons and your appointed feasts my soul hates; they have become a burden to me, I am weary of bearing them. When you spread forth your hands, I will hide my eyes from you; even though you make many prayers, I will not listen*" (Isaiah 1:12-15). Were it to end there it would be horrible. However, it does not end there. The gracious Lord of heaven says, "*Wash yourselves, make yourselves clean, remove the evil of your doings from my eyes, cease to do evil, learn to do good; seek justice, correct oppression; defend the fatherless, plead for the widow*" (Isaiah 1:16-17). As I write this, I pray for myself as I pray for the Church that at no point will our prayers become a burden to God.

PRIDE

We must put off all obstacles to prayer, but may we never get to the point where we think that God has been made our debtor. We should never bring any elements of self-righteousness before God, for they will cause Him to hide His face from us. The Bible says, "*There they cry out, but He does not answer, because of the pride of evil men. Surely God does not hear an empty cry, nor does the Almighty regard it*" (Job 35:12-13). The self-righteous Pharisee went away unblessed, but the humble and penitent Publican was blessed!

GOD AND THE PRAYERS OF THE RIGHTEOUS

The Lord is committed to answering the prayers of the righteous. The Word of God says, *"If you will seek God and make supplication to the Almighty, if you are pure and upright, surely then He will rouse Himself for you and reward you with a rightful habitation"* (Job 8:5-6). *"But know that the Lord has set apart the godly for Himself. The Lord hears when I call to Him"* (Psalms 4:3). *"The eyes of the Lord are toward the righteous, and His ears toward their cry"* (Psalms 34:15). *"The Lord is far from the wicked, but He hears the prayers of the righteous"* (Proverb 15:29). *"We know that God does not listen to sinners, but if anyone is a worshipper of God and does His will, God listens to him"* (John 9:31). *"For the eyes of the Lord are upon the righteous and His ears are open to their prayer"* (1 Peter 3:12).

"Beloved, if our hearts do not condemn us, we have confidence before God; and we receive from Him whatever we ask, because we keep His commandments and do what pleases Him" (1 John 3:21-22).

Such promises should stir the saint to make holiness his aim and prayer his life.

CHAPTER 7

Praise and thanksgiving

PRAISE AS PART OF PRAYER

We have said that prayer aims not only at asking and receiving from the Lord but more so as communion with the Lord. The ultimate purpose of redemption is to produce a people unto God who have total and continuous communion with God. It is to produce a people who are perfectly satisfied with God and in God and a people in whom God delights in a complete sense. The psalmist expressed this satisfaction in God in the following words, "*I have looked upon Thee in the sanctuary, beholding Thy power and Thy glory. Because Thy steadfast love is better than life, my lips will praise Thee. So I will bless Thee as long as I live; I will lift up my hands and call upon Thy name. My soul is feasted as with marrow and fat, and my mouth praises Thee with joyful lips*" (Psalms 63:2-5). "*How precious to me are Thy thoughts, O God! How vast is the sum of them! If I would count them, they are more than the sand. When I awake, I am still with Thee*" (Psalms 139:17-18). Words like these are expressions of deep communion, yet let us remember that those who are able to fully enter into that kind of deep communion are those who can truly say, "*O God, Thou are my God, I seek Thee, my soul thirsts for Thee; my flesh faints for Thee, as a dry and weary land wherever no water is*" (Psalms 63:1). When a person begins to thirst, seek, and faint after God, it will not be long before the praise that comes out of a fulfilled heart flows from his heart to God.

Praise is the exalting, extolling, blessing, glorifying, worshiping of the Lord God, primarily for whom He is and, in a secondary way, for what He has done, while thanksgiving is directed to God mainly for what He has done.

God deserves to be praised. He has clearly shown us Himself — in His creation and finally in His Son. We know Him enough to praise Him. The praises that are due to God can be divided into four classes :

First of all, praise is due to Him from those who know and love Him.

Secondly, praise is due to Him from all of the inanimate creation.

Thirdly, praise is due to Him from all who are on earth.

And, lastly, praise is due to Him from all in heaven. We shall look at praise, as depicted by the Bible, as coming from these four classes. Then we shall look at the eternality of praise, praise in public worship, and the implications of this for the praying saint.

PRAISE DUE TO GOD FROM ALL WHO KNOW AND LOVE HIM

Moses and the people of Israel expressed their praises in a song that ran in part like this: "*I will sing to the Lord, for He has triumphed gloriously; the horse and his rider he has thrown into the sea. The Lord is my strength and my song, and He has become my salvation; this is my God and I will praise Him*" (Exodus 15:12). Another song of praise came from the lips of Deborah and Barak, who sang saying, "*Hear, O kings: give ear, O princes; to the Lord I will sing, I will make melody to the Lord, the God of Israel*" (Judges 5:3). Isaiah said, "*Sing praises to the Lord, for He has done gloriously, let this be known in all the earth. Shout, and sing for joy, O inhabitant of Zion, for great in your midst is the Holy One of Israel*" (Isaiah 12:5-6). Mary said, "*My soul magnifies the Lord, and my spirit rejoices in God my Saviour*" (Luke 1:46-47).

However, it is David the psalmist who excelled in praising the Lord and in inviting all others to do the same. He must have lived a life that was intimately in fellowship with the Lord. He must have loved the Lord deeply. His eyes must have been opened to the glory of the Lord as the eyes of few others have ever been. Let us look at what he said about praise and pray that the Lord may teach us to go and do likewise.

"*For this I will extol Thee, O Lord, among the nations, and sing praise to Thy name*" (2 Samuel 22:50). "*Sing to Him, sing praises to Him, tell of all His wonderful works! Glory in His Holy name; let the hearts of those who seek the Lord rejoice"* (1 Chronicles 16:9-10). *"Ascribe to the Lord the glory due His name; bring an offering and come before Him! Worship the Lord in holy array"* (1 Chronicles 16:28-29). *"I will give to the Lord the thanks due to His righteousness, and I will sing praises to the name of the Lord, the Most High"* (Psalms 7:17). *"O Lord, our Lord, how majestic is Thy name in all the earth!"* (Psalms 8:1). *"I will be glad and exult in Thee; I will sing praises to Thy name, O Most High"* (Psalms 9:2). *"Be exalted, O Lord, in Thy strength! We will sing and praise Thy power"* (Psalms 21:13). *"O magnify the Lord with me, and let us exalt His name together"* (Psalms 34:3). *"Sing praises to God, sing praises! Sing praises! For God is the King of all the earth; sing praises with a psalm"* (Psalms 47:6-7). *"O Lord, open then my lips and my mouth shall show forth and make melody! Awake, O harp and lyre! I will awake the dawn! I will give thanks to Thee, O Lord, among the peoples; I will sing praises to Thee among the nations. For Thy steadfast love is great to the heavens, Thy faithfulness to the clouds. Be exalted, O God above the heavens! Let Thy glory be over all the earth"* (Psalms 57:8-11). *"Make a joyful noise to God, all the earth, sing the glory of His name; give to Him glorious praise! Say to God, how terrible are Thy deeds! So great is Thy power that Thy enemies cringe before Thee. All the earth worships Thee; they sing praises to Thee, sing praises to Thy name"* (Psalms 66:1-4). *"My mouth will tell of Thy righteous acts, of Thy deeds of salvation all the day, for their number is past my knowledge. With the mighty deeds of the Lord God I will come, I will praise Thy righteousness, Thine alone. O God, from my youth Thou hast taught me, and I still proclaim Thy wondrous deeds. So even to old age and gray hairs, O God, do not forsake me, till I proclaim Thy might to all the generations to come. Thy power and Thy righteousness, O God, reach the high heaven. Thou who hast done great things, O God, who is like Thee?"* (Psalms 71:15-19). *"Seven times a day I praise Thee for Thy righteous ordinances"* (Psalms 119:164). *"I give Thee thanks, O Lord, with my whole heart; before the gods I sing Thy praise. I bow down toward Thy holy temple and give thanks to Thy name for Thy steadfast love and Thy faithfulness, for Thou hast exalted above everything Thy name and Thy Word"* (Psalms 138:1-2). *"Praise the Lord! Praise the Lord, O my soul! I will praise the Lord*

as long as I live; I will sing praises to my God while I have being"
(Psalms 146:1-2).

So the whole of the psalmist's life was wrapped up in praise. He
walked close to God. He saw God's glory. He experienced God's deliverance and God's goodness to him so much that he could not
contain himself. He overflowed with praise. He was not content to
praise alone. He invited all who could do so to join him.

Praise due from inanimate creation

God deserves praise not only from those who know Him. He
deserves praise from inanimate creation, which having no will of its
own, fulfils all His desire for it. The Bible says, *"Let the sea roar, and
all that fills it, let the field exult, and everything it! Then shall the trees
of the wood sing for joy before the Lord, for He comes to judge the earth"*
(1 Chronicles 16:32-33). *"Let heaven and earth praise Him, the seas and
everything that moves therein"* (Psalms 69:34).

*"Let the sea roar, and all that fill it; the world and those who dwell in
it! Let the floods clap their hands; let the hills sing for joy together before
the Lord, for He comes to judge the earth!"* (Psalms 98:7-9).

*"Praise the Lord from the heart, you sea monsters and all deeps, fire
and hail, snow and frost, stormy wind fulfilling His command! Mountains
and all hills, fruit trees and all cedars! Beasts and all cattle, creeping things
and flying birds! Let them praise the name of the Lord, for His name alone
is exalted; His glory is above earth and heaven"* (Psalms 148:7-13).
*"Sing, O heavens, for the Lord has done it, shout O depths of the earth,
break forth into singing, O mountains, O forest, and every tree in it! For
the Lord has redeemed Jacob and will glorified in Israel"* (Isaiah 44:23).
*"For you shall go out in joy, and be led forth in peace; the mountains and
the hills before you shall break forth into singing, and all the trees of the
field shall clap their hands"* (Isaiah 55:12).

When next you hear the sound of praise from trees, lightening, birds around, join them in praising the Lord. I have often been humbled and motivated to further praise when I thought that if I did not praise my Lord, stones and the rest would do it. I have often been humbled by the fact that He could put me aside and receive praise from the rest of creation. O Lord, do not cast me away. Give me the privilege of praising you now and throughout all eternity.

Praise due from all on earth

There is a sense in which the heart of God is not satisfied until all of His creation praises Him. The purpose of redemption in the fullest sense and to the fullest extent is that all of creation shall praise Him unceasingly. Praise is due to the Lord from all on earth. The Bible says, *"Clap your hands, all peoples! Shout to God with loud songs of joy"* (Psalms 47:1). *"Make a joyful noise to God, all the earth; sing the glory of His name"* (Psalms 66:1-2). *"All the earth worships Thee; they sing praises to Thee, sing praises to Thy name"* (Psalms 66:4). *"Let the peoples praise Thee, O God; let all the peoples praise Thee"* (Psalms 67:3). *"O sing to the Lord a new song; sing to the Lord, all the earth!"* (Psalms 96:1) *"Praise the Lord, all nations! Extol Him, all peoples!"* (Psalms 117:1). *"Let everything that breathes praise the Lord! Praise the Lord"* (Psalms 150:6). Praise is not only due from all on earth, it is due all the time. The Bible says, *"From the rising of the sun to its setting the name of the Lord is to be praised!"* (Psalms 113:3). All time is praise time. Praise should not depend on our moods or our circumstances. It is to be given to the Lord all the time. If you are on earth and not yet praising God all the time you are subnormal. How can a praying saint fail to praise the Lord ?

PRAISE DUE FROM ALL IN HEAVEN

The Word of God says, *"Praise the Lord! Praise the Lord from the heavens, praise Him in the heights! Praise Him, all His angels; praise Him, all His hosts"* (Psalms 148:1-2). *"And suddenly there was with the angel a multitude of the heavenly host praising God and saying, 'Glory to God in the highest, and on earth peace among men with whom He is pleased!'* (Luke 2:13-14). *"Then I looked, and I heard around the throne and the living creatures and the elders the voice of many angels, numbering myriads of myriads and thousands of thousands, saying with a loud voice, "Worthy is the lamb who was slain, to receive power and wealth and wisdom and might and honour and glory and blessing!" And I hear every creature in heaven and on earth and under the earth and in the sea, and all therein, saying "To Him who sits upon the throne and to the lamb be blessing and honour and glory and might for ever and ever!"'* (Revelation 5:11-13). *"And all the angels stood round the elders and the four living creatures, and they fell on their faces before the throne and worshipped God, saying, 'Amen! Blessing and glory and wisdom and thanksgiving and honour and power and might be to our God for ever and ever! Amen'"* (Revelation 7:11-12). *"After this I heard what seemed to be the loud voice of a great multitude in heaven, crying 'Hallelujah! Salvation and glory and power belong to our God"* (Revelation 19:1). All of heaven is caught up in praise. Can we afford not to join them? Angles and all the mighty hosts of heaven consider it a privilege to praise Him. Do you, too, consider it so?

THE ETERNALITY OF PRAISE

Many things that we do here for the Lord will end when this era has waned away: Tongues will cease; prophecies will all have been fulfilled; et cetera. One of the few thing that shall never end, be it in the millennial reign of Christ or in the Kingdom, is praise. Praise shall continue throughout all eternity. If we do not mature in praise here, we shall be truly deficient there. May God help to heal all our deficiencies in praise now. About the fact that praise shall continue, the Bible says, *"I will bless the Lord at all times; His praises shall continually be in my mouth"* (Psalms 34:1). *"But I will rejoice for ever, I will sing praises to the God of Jacob"* (Psalms 75:9). *"I give thanks to Thee, O Lord my God, with my whole heart; I will glorify Thy name for ever"* (Psalms 86:12). *"But we will bless the Lord from this time forth and for evermore. Praise the Lord"* (Psalms 115:18). *"I will extol Thee, my God and King, and bless Thy name for ever and ever. Every day I will bless Thee, and praise Thy name for ever and ever"* (Psalms 145:1-2).

PRAISE AS PART OF PUBLIC WORSHIP

Praise is not only for private prayer. It is also for public worship. The Bible says, *"Then I will thank Thee in the great congregation; in the mighty throng I will praise Thee"* (Psalms 35:18). *"Bless God in the great congregation, the Lord, O you who are of Israel's fountain"* (Psalms 68:26). *"Enter His gates with thanksgiving, and His courts with praise! Give thanks to Him, bless His name!"* (Psalms 100:4). *"Let them extol Him in the congregation of the people, and praise Him in the assembly of the elders"* (Psalms 107:32). *"Praise the Lord. Praise the name of the Lord; give praise, O servants of the Lord, you that stand in the house of the Lord, in the courts of the house of our God! Praise the Lord, for the Lord is good; sing to His name, for He is gracious"* (Psalms 135:1-3).

Praise is to be an indispensable part of the worship of a local assembly. Time is to be set apart for it and the redeemed for the Lord given an opportunity to lift up their voices to the Lord their God. Every prayer meeting ought to have some portion of it set aside for praise. There is no substitute for this.

HOW TO PRAISE THE LORD

Many believers will say, "Now I know that praise is important, but how do I go about it?" Let us first insist that to praise the Lord is a command that must be obeyed. Disobedience is as deadly a sin as all other sins. Secondly, let us insist that praise is for all the time and from all places. Thirdly, let us state that everything that can be used to praise Him should be used - the trumpet, the guitar, the drum, and every kind of musical instrument. We are to use our voices to shout out His praise and our hands to clap out to Him. We can dance our praises.

Praise is often spontaneous, but we cannot leave it to the moments when we feel like doing so. We are to praise Him even if all of our flesh rebels against praising Him.

Praise is not just shouting, I praise you, I bless you, I worship you, I magnify you, I glorify you, et cetera, good as this may be and is. We praise Him for His glorious person, who He is: His holiness, His purity, His kindness, His love, and for every wonderful attribute of His unequalled and incomparable being. Have a notebook where you record all the wondrous attributes of God, Father, Son, and Holy Spirit. Begin to praise Him for the attributes you have discovered so far and He will reveal Himself more to you so that you can worship Him even more. You will then have a growing record as you grow in praise.

We also praise Him for His mighty acts. Here we begin with thanksgiving and end in praise, and there is no room for separating the two. Make a list of all the mighty acts of God in creation, redemption, et cetera. Also include His goodness to you as an individual. His Goodness to the local church, to the whole Church, et cetera, and you will soon have a long list of praise topics. Make sure that you do not only make a list but that you actually take time for praising the Lord. All of prayer ought to begin with praise!

SEASONS OF PRAISE

I strongly recommend that each believer and each local assembly should set aside some special times for praise. What of a week, a month when all of prayer is praise (no asking, no interceding, et cetera). This will raise the spiritual level of the believer and the Church. If it is right to plan other areas of praise, it is even more important that we plan praise, for the devil will do everything possible to stop us from praising. Praise humiliates and destroys him as nothing else does. It forces him to withdraw, for who can stand unhindered praise being lavished on his enemy?

FINALLY

Please, praise the Lord. Again I say, praise the Lord. Remember, praise is a vocal acknowledgement, a vocal establishment of that which already is the greatness of God. Let praise become, not only a temporary upshot in the moments of bliss, but a way of life for you. A PRAYER LIFE THAT LACKS THE INGREDIENTS OF PRAISE MAY BE CORRECT BUT IT WILL LACK SWEETNESS AND JOY. IT WILL BE LIKE UNSPICED FOOD. GOD WILL ACCEPT SUCH PRAYERS, BUT THEY WILL NOT SATISFY HIS HEART!

THANKSGIVING IN PRAYER

The Lord Jesus expressed disappointment at the fact that of the ten lepers that He healed on one occasion, only one returned to express gratitude. God expects gratitude from us for all that we receive from Him. The average believer is more committed to asking for things from the Lord and not to giving thanks. This ought not to be so. As we look at the matter of thanksgiving as a part of the prayer life of the normal believer, let us repent of the ingratitude of our former lives and seek to be cleansed for such a sin.

EXHORTATION TO THANKSGIVING

"O give thanks to the Lord, call on His name, make known His deeds among the people!" (1Chronicles 16:8) *"It is good to give thanks to the Lord"* (Psalms 92:1). *"Let us come into His presence with thanksgiving: let us make a joyful noise to Him with songs of praise! For God is a great God and a great King above all gods"* (Psalms 95:2-3). *"O give thanks to the Lord, call on His name, make known His deeds among the people"* (Psalms 105:1). *"Addressing one another in psalms and hymns and spiritual songs, singing and making melody to the Lord with all your heart, and always and for everything giving thanks in the name of our Lord Jesus Christ to God the Father"* (Ephesians 5:19-20). *"Give thanks in all circumstances; for this is the will of God in Christ Jesus for you"* (1 Thessalonians 5:18). It is obvious then that the Word of God calls us to give thanks to God in the name of Christ FOR EVERYTHING, IN ALL CIRCUMSTANCES, ALWAYS, FOR THIS IS THE WILL OF GOD FOR US. We repeat, God's will for the redeemed is that they will give thanks to God in the name of Jesus ALWAYS, FOR EVERYTHING, IN ALL CIRCUMSTANCES. If we do not so give thanks, we fail in fulfilling God's will. It is not for us humans to decide whether thanks are to be given to God in a particular circumstance or not. God has taken that right from us and has decreed that thanks be given to Him for EVERY CIRCUMSTANCE AND ALWAYS. It may look horrible. We may not be able to see God in it. We may be baffled, but one thing we must do, we must give thanks, at least out of obedience. Even if the circumstance is a work of the Enemy, let us remember that he is not God. God permitted him to so act, and God will use that which looks ho-

peless to work out something wonderful for His glory and our conformity to the image of His dear Son. The betrayal by Judas was horrible, but God used it to work out our salvation. The selling off of Joseph by his brethren was terrible, but God used it to preserve much life. The attitude of Potiphar's wife was exceedingly sinful, but God used it to bring Joseph to premiership in Egypt. I repeat, God is working out His wondrous purposes. Nothing is outside His control. There is no circumstance that He cannot and will not turn into the good of those who love Him.

In order that God should turn all circumstances for the welfare of His children and the building up of His Kingdom, He demands the co-operation of His blood-bought children. He will temporarily allow some circumstance untransformed into good if He does not have our co-operation. This co-operation is given when we thank Him. Thanksgiving is another special ingredient that speeds the train of God's will on its journeys. May we be determined to co-operate. The devil will attack thanksgiving with full force. However, he is impotent against believers who know their grounds and who maintain them by praise and thanksgiving.

Thanksgiving was given in scripture for some situations. We shall look at some of these.

THANKSGIVING FOR CHRIST AND HIS SALVATION

Zacharias, upon being filled with the Holy Spirit, prophesied during his praise and thanksgiving saying, *"Blessed be the Lord of Israel, for He has visited and has redeemed His people, and has raised up a horn of salvation for us in the house of His servant David"* (Luke 1:68-69). The apostle Paul said, *"But thanks be to God who gives us the victory through our Lord Jesus Christ"* (1 Corinthians 15:7). *"But thanks be to God who in Christ always leads us to triumph, and through us spreads the fragrance of the knowledge of Him everywhere*" (2 Corinthians 2:14). "*Thanks be to God for this inexpressible gift*" (2 Corinthians 9:15). "*Blessed be the God and Father of our Lord Jesus Christ who has blessed us in Christ with every spiritual blessing in the heavenly places*" (Ephesians 1:3). "*Giving thanks to the Father, who has qualified us to share in the inheritance of the saints in light*" (Colossians 1:12). The apostle Peter wrote, "*Blessed be the God and Father of our Lord Jesus Christ! By His great mercy we have been born anew to a living hope through the resurrection of Jesus Christ from the dead*" (1 Peter 1:3).

We thank God readily for our salvation and for the death of Christ on the cross. We find it easy because we now see what this has worked out for us. It needed great faith to stand there by the cross and thank God for the nails that were being driven into His Son; yet the men of vision could thank God even for that, knowing that even that would be turned by God into a blessing.

There should never be a situation when a believer runs out of topics for praise and thanksgiving. The mighty work of God through Christ will always be there to thank Him for, the application of that work to us as individuals will always be there. So we should never run out of thanksgiving subjects. Have you ever thanked God for the one who brought you to know Him ? Have you ever thanked Him for all that He has done in you to bring you so far in your walk with Him? Have you ever thanked Him enough for all the times that He has forgiven you and cleansed you? Have you ever thanked Him for the local assembly and the privilege of being a part of it? As you look into the future fully assured that the Lord will keep you faithful in Christ until the end, that you will by His grace be raptured, that you will sit at the marriage supper with Him, that you will reign with Him, et cetera, have you ever thanked Him enough for these and the millions of other spiritual blessings too numerous to write down ?

THANKSGIVING FOR THE FULFILLMENT OF PROMISE

It is a wonderful thing when God fulfils His promises. Not that He is capable of failure to do so, but such acts on His part ought to raise forth great thanksgiving from His elect. There are many such examples in Scripture. Solomon said, "*Blessed be the Lord, the God of Israel, who with His hand has fulfilled what He promised with His mouth to my father David*" (1 Kings 8:15). He further said, "*Blessed be the Lord who has given rest to His people Israel, according to all that He promised; not one Word has failed of all His good promises which He uttered by Moses His servant*" (1 Kings 8:56). Daniel's hymn of thanksgiving was, "*Blessed be the name of God for ever and ever, to whom belongs wisdom and might. He changes times and seasons; He removes kings; He gives wisdom to the wise and knowledge to those who have understanding; He reveals deep and mysterious things; He knows what is in darkness, and the light dwells with Him. To Thee, O God of my fathers, I give thanks and praise for Thou has given me wisdom and strength, and hast now made known to me what we asked of Thee, for Thou has made known to us the King's matter*" (Daniel 2.20-23).

Which of God's promises has He fulfilled in your life? Did you make a record of them? Have you thanked the Lord for them?

THANKSGIVING FOR DELIVERANCE FROM ENEMIES

Jethro said, "*Blessed be the Lord, who has delivered you out of the hands of the Egyptians and out of the hand of Pharaoh*" (Exodus 18:10). Jehoshaphat was once in difficulty with his enemies. He prayed to the Lord and had the assurance that the Lord would fight for him. What did he do after that? He did not wait to see the victory. He "*bowed his head with his face to the ground, and all Judah and the inhabitants of Jerusalem fell down before the Lord, worshipping the Lord. And the Levites... stood up to praise the Lord, the God of Israel with a very loud voice... He appointed those who were to sing to the Lord and praise Him in holy array as they went before the army and said, 'Give thanks to the Lord, for His steadfast love endures for ever'"* (2 Chronicles 20:18-21). This all must have looked stupid to the enemy – thanksgiving before war. It must have looked even more ridiculous, an army led by singers. Yes, that is God's way, and His ways often seem foolish to carnal minds. But listen: *"and when they began to sing and praise, the Lord set an ambush against the men of Ammon, Moab, and Mount Seir, who had come against Judah so that they were routed"* (2 Chronicles 20:22). From God's point of view, everything was ready for Judah to be granted victory, but God would not act until that final catalyst of thanksgiving came. Immediately it came, victory also came. We insist that there are many things that God is waiting for our praise and thanksgiving to bring to pass. The praising, thanksgiving people will see God's fullest victories.

When victory was thus granted they yet assembled to bless the Lord. The Bible says, *"On the fourth day, they assembled in the Valley of Berachah, for there they blessed the Lord"* (2 Chronicles 20:26).

Nehemiah also arranged a great ceremony of giving thanks. He arranged those who gave thanks in two processions, *"And they offered great sacrifices that day and rejoiced, for God had made them rejoice with great joy"* (Nehemiah 12:31-43).

David gave thanks all the time. He said, *"I will rejoice and be glad for Thy steadfast love, because Thou has seen my affliction, Thou has taken heed of my adversities, and has not delivered me into the hand of the enemy; Thou has set my feet in a broad place"* (Psalms 31:7-8).

A PRAYER FORMULA

In the natural realm, we want to give thanks for that which we have received. In the supernatural realm, things work differently. We are to ask, thank, receive, and then thank again. We have seen that that was the case with Jehoshaphat. He asked and thanked, then received and thanked. Paul teaches the same thing. He says, *"Have no anxiety about anything but in everything by prayer and supplication with thanksgiving let your requests be made known to God"* (Philippians 4:6). We should thank the Lord shortly after we have made our request known to Him because we know that He will grant the desires of our hearts. When thanksgiving accompanies requests, that shows deep confidence in the Lord, confidence that God always rewards. After the request has been granted, we should again turn to the Lord in thanksgiving. The first thanksgiving before seeing, the second after seeing.

COSTLY THANKSGIVING

There will be times when we do not at all feel like thanking God, times when we will feel it easier to break than to give thanks. At such moments let us all the more give thanks. Let us say to ourselves, "Whether you like it or not, you are to give thanks," and let us act on this declaration.

Some thanksgivings comes from moments of joy, but all moments in the walk of faith are not like that. There will be the dark of deepest agony when we face our personal Gethsemane. We must still give thanks then. At such moments, thanksgiving becomes a sacrifice, a very costly sacrifice. The Lord wants such sacrifices. He says, *"He who brings thanksgiving as his sacrifice honours me"* (Psalms 50:23). Yes, thanksgiving is a costly sacrifice. Furthermore, *"So Jesus suffered outside the gate in order to sanctify the people through His own blood. Therefore let us go forth to Him outside the camp, and bear the abuse He endured. For here we have no lasting city, but we seek the city which is to come. Through Him then let us continually offer up a sacrifice of praise to God, that is the fruit of lips that acknowledge His name"* (Hebrews 13:12-15). Jesus, our supreme example, offered up such sacrifices to the Father. He had done many mighty works in Chorazin and Bethsaida, and these cities had refused to repent. It must have hurt Him deeply. What did He do? He offered a sacrifice of praise and thanksgiving. He said, *"I thank Thee Father Lord of heaven and earth, that Thou hast hidden these things from the wise and understanding and revealed them to babes; yea, Father, for such was Thy gracious will"* (Matthew 11:25-26). When Job lost everything, what did he do? He fell down and worshipped, and He said, *"Blessed be the name of the Lord"* (Job 1:21). This is most precious in God's sight.

SEASONS OF THANKSGIVING

As we have said, with praise there should also be seasons of thanksgiving. These would be times set apart by individuals and by the local assembly for giving thanks to the Lord. David ____
a day of thanksgiving (1 Chronicles 16:7). Should we not

Since thanksgiving is also aimed at publishing the goodness of our God, should we not do it in an elaborate way? Should we not plan how best to carry it out and then carry it out?

FINALLY

"Thanksgiving shall continue for ever" (Psalms 30:12, 44:8). *"Continue steadfastly in prayer, watching therein with thanksgiving"* (Colossians 4:2). The mature saints in the Kingdom will be those who have made the most progress now in thanksgiving! Praise be to the Lord!!

CHAPTER 8

Importunity

The Lord Jesus stressed the necessity for importunity in prayer if one is to prevail with God. Importunity is persistence in prayer until God answers the prayer, however long it would take for Him to answer. It is the determination to hold on to God and not to let Him go until He answers.

Jacob of old persisted. The Bible says, *"And Jacob was left alone; and a man wrestled with him until the breaking of the day. When the man saw that he did not prevail against Jacob, he touched the hollow of his thigh; and Jacob's thigh was put out of joint as he wrestled with him. Then he said, 'Let me go, for the day is breaking.' But Jacob said, 'I will not let you go, unless you bless me.' And he said to him, 'What is your name?' And he said 'Jacob' Then he said, 'Your name shall no more be called Jacob, but Israel (prince of God), for you have striven with God and with men, and have prevailed' "* (Genesis 32:24-28).

Importunity is the wrestling with God, not just childlike praying. It is a conflict. It is fighting for victory. It is fighting persistently until victory is won. The man wrestled with Jacob. Jacob wrestled in return. He was determined to have his way. The angel did not want Jacob to have the victory, so he dislocated his thigh to cause him to yield. Jacob did not yield. He wrestled even more violently and set out his conditions for releasing the angel; he must receive blessing first. The angel was reluctant, more or less unwilling to bless. He, however, wanted to go away from Jacob's entanglement in wrestling before the break of day. He was now in a dilemma. Jacob said, "Bless me and then you can go away free. If not you will just stay here". So, you see the angel's dilemma; bless Jacob and go free, or stay fighting with an unbending Jacob. The angel did not want the day to break on him in a fight with an unyielding, undefeatable man. So he took the other alternative. He blessed him and made him a prince of God. He did not become a prince of God by simple prayer.

The Lord Jesus importuned in prayer. He encourages people to engage in this kind of praying. *"He told them a parable, to the effect that they ought always to pray and not lose heart. He said, 'In a certain city there was a judge who neither feared God nor regarded man; and there was a widow in that city who KEPT COMING TO HIM and saying, "Vindicate me against my adversary." For A WHILE HE REFUSED, but afterwards he said to himself, "though I neither fear God nor regard man, yet BECAUSE THIS WIDOW BOTHERS ME I WILL VINDICATE HER OR SHE WILL WEAR ME OUT WITH HER CONTINUAL COMING." And the Lord said, 'Hear what the unrighteous judge says. And will not God vindicate His elect, who cry to Him day and night? WILL HE DELAY LONG OVER THEM? I tell you, He will vindicate them speedily. Nevertheless, when the Son of man comes, will He find faith on earth?'* "(Luke 18:1-8).

This woman had an adversary. We have an adversary, the devil. Things were not going fine with her because of the frequent and annoying attacks of the Enemy. It is as if the Enemy never let her free. She could not continue in that kind of situation. Today in the Church, the devil is actively at work. He is attacking God's work and God's people right and left. He knows that his time is limited; therefore he wants to do the greatest harm possible before his hour is over. The question is, Why are so many of God's children living in such unconsciousness of the devil's attack? I think there are a number of reasons for this. One reason is that their lives are spiritually so impotent that the devil sees no reason in harassing them. They live as if they belonged to the devil. They are no threat to hell so that Satan sees no reason for bothering them. So he leaves them at ease, undisturbed. Another reason is that some believers are living so perpetually in sin and at such a distance from the Lord that they cannot "feel" the pains of the kingdom. Their spiritual senses have been so dulled by sin that they cannot even "feel" the violence of the kingdom. A third reason is that through ignorance of the Word, many believers blame the devil's attacks on circumstances, "bad luck," and the like, and fail to see the one behind the system. Also, those believers who are either in love or are infatuated with this world will not know from experience the violence that the kingdom faces.

There are, however, some believers (they may not be many, but they are there) who pose the greatest threats to the wicked one, and so he attacks them relentlessly and mercilessly, to destroy them at once if it were possible. Such believers are captains in God's army. In normal warfare, one aims at destroying field marshals, generals, captains, and the like. Who would specialize in destroying recruits? Who would waste a bullet on a weak or crippled or dying soldier? The woman in the parable was important. She was having severe attacks. There was only one person who could vindicate her – the judge. Unfortunately for her, the judge was unwilling. When she first came, he refused. He might have said, "Go away. I have no time for you." She went away but her problem remained. Her adversary was still a bother to her. She went back to the judge and the judge would not listen. If she had another way of seeking relief, she might gladly have had it, but she had none. Her deliverance lay with the judge. So she went back. Then the judge reckoned, saying, "I have no desire to be of service to this woman. However, she has become a problem to me. If I do not vindicate her, I will have no peace." So he decided to vindicate her. He did it afterwards, when it was necessary for his own peace.

The Lord Jesus taught that God was like the wicked judge, not in wickedness or in reluctance, but in a capacity of being moved by persistence. God delights in answering the prayers of those who persist in asking. There is something in the heart of God that responds to persistence in prayer. God is not unwilling. In fact He will vindicate His elect SPEEDILY. He is anxious to vindicate His elect. He will not waste time. One question, however, arises, Which elect will He vindicate speedily? He will vindicate the elect who, under trial by the enemy, cry to Him day and night.

Many believers have never cried to God; so they will never have the type of answers that are produced by God responding to tears. Some shed an occasional tear but wipe it off and keep going as if there never was any weeping. Where are those who will weep night and day? Where are those who will not allow their tears to be wiped off by any other person or thing except the Lord? The Lord, indeed, vindicates. When He sees tears flowing from faces night and day, He will rush to our rescue. He will deal with the Enemy and secure our freedom. Sometimes the Lord does delay. He waits to see if we have come to the point where we will not seek another answer but wait on Him. In such cases, will He delay long? No! No! He will not. He will act.

The importance of importunity is so great that the Lord was prepared to teach even further on it. He said, "*Which of you who has a friend will go to him at midnight and say to him, 'Friend, lend me three loaves; for a friend of mine has arrived on a journey and I have nothing to set before him', and he will answer from within, 'Do not bother me; the door is now shut, my children are with me in bed; I cannot get up and give you anything'? I tell you though he will not get up and give him anything because he is his friend, yet because of his importunity, he will rise and give him whatever he needs*" (Luke 11:5-8).

Here, as we have already seen, there is a man in difficulty – in trouble. He is stranded. He cannot solve an urgent problem himself. He has a friend. He knows that the friend is able to provide the answer which he so badly needs. Unfortunately for him, the hour is late, very late; almost too late. If he could postpone his need, he would gladly have done so, but he could not. He had a visitor with an empty stomach who had to have something to eat. It was embarrassing that he had nothing for his visitor. What must he do? He had only one choice. He had to overcome the barrier that was raised by the late hour. He had to go to his friend even though it was midnight.

He found that the friend would have given him bread but for the following four obstacles:

1.   It was too late – midnight.

2.   The door was shut and possibly locked, and it was probably that kind of door which, when once shut, took much pains to open.

3.   He was already in bed. It would have been easier if he were still up. He had changed into his night garments. Meeting his need would involve possibly an undesirable change of clothes.

4.   He was not alone in bed. His children were there. Possibly they were already asleep and maybe his children were that kind who, when woken up, would cry and find it difficult to sleep again. If they woke up, as they would certainly do if he woke up to give bread to his friend, sleep for them and for himself might be jeopardized for the whole night.

After considering all these factors, the friend seemed to have been saying, I love you. You are my friend, but it is impossible. You are a bother.

THE IMPOSSIBLE BECOMES POSSIBLE

The friend outside heard all these reasonable excuses. He understood that his friend was being nasty or unreasonable. He saw with him; but he looked at his need that could not be postponed and he decided that he would persist and thereby make the impossible possible. He continued to ask and knock. It got to a point where the friend inside the house felt that the worst that he feared - his children being awakened - was about to happen anyway (because of the persistent knocks).   He decided that he should get up, give the man what he wanted, and have peace.   The Bible says that *"He will rise and give him whatever he needs"* (Luke 11:8).   Maybe that the friend having woken up would give him not only the loaves of bread but also some fish and some drinks.

THE INTENSIFICATION OF PERSISTENCE

The Lord went on to say, "*Ask, and it will be given to you; seek, and you will find; knock and it will be opened to you*" (Luke 11:9). The Lord was saying, "*Ask and keep on asking and you will receive.*" Intensify this, go beyond just asking, seek as you ask. Seek and keep on seeking and you will find. And go even deeper in seeking. Let seeking give way to knocking – fierce deliberate asking and seeking. What will not give way to asking will give way to seeking, and if need be knocking has to be done.

The Lord further said, "*For everyone who asks receives, and he who seeks finds, and to him who knocks it will be opened*" (Luke 11:10). There is, therefore, no reason why anyone should ask and not receive. If a person were to ask and not receive it would most likely be because he did not ask persistently. If he sought and did not find, it could be because he sought superficially, for too short a time, and gave up. If he knocked and it was not opened to him, it could be that he walked away just as the Lord was just about to open to him.

There are believers whose prayer life is at the level of asking. They receive what is available at the asking plane. They will receive all that is available at the asking plane if they fulfil the conditions for having prayer answered and persist in asking until the answer comes.

The asking plane is the elementary plane. All begin there. But it is not the only plane. Beyond the asking plane is the seeking plane. Seeking is more intense action. The seeking plane is the plane of greater intensity. It is the plane of beginning warfare in prayer. No one can seek passively. Many things that cannot be received by asking and continuing in asking will be obtained by the seeker. Seeking is more determined effort. A person can ask and not receive and then go away calmly. However, if he were to seek in prayer and not find, he would be totally frustrated. Few believers pray on this plane. It is costly, for one must know something on laying hold of God to make progress here.

There is yet the knocking plane. This is the prayer plane of violence in the spiritual world. The Lord was praying at this plane in the garden of Gethsemane. It was intense. It was violent. It produced sweat like drops of blood.

It was not child play. Praying at this plane means that the total man-spirit, soul and body, is engaged in prayer. Were God to fail to answer at that plane, the praying person would be finished permanently. It is the plane of no return, beyond which the person can pray no further and wrestle no further but rest in the perfect will of God.

The will of God ought to be known before any kind of praying is engaged in; but there is a knowledge of the will of God, revealed to those who would go through persistence in asking, seeking, and enduring the fierceness of the battle, of knocking night and day with tears and groans for a season. To such praying saints, God unveils His will in a way that others will not be allowed to know and from that revelation comes perfect peace.

IMPORTUNITY A KEY TO KNOWING GOD'S PERFECT WILL

It can be said of the Lord Jesus that He entered Gethsemane knowing God's will. He came out of it knowing God's will and being united with that perfect will. There is a sense in which it can be said of the Lord that something deep and very far-reaching took place in Him in that garden. He went to the garden knowing that He had to die. He came out of the garden ready to die. He came to the garden horrified by the sinfulness of sin. He went out of the garden identified fully with sin. The mighty importunate praying made the difference. He was different as He came out – no more questions, only a deep willingness, a surpassing joy that the cross was the Father's will for Him and He was about to carry it and die on it.

A WORD TO THE WOULD-BE STUDENT IN THE SCHOOL OF IMPORTUNATE PRAYING

God is calling a band of overcomers to co-operate with Him to a degree that He is not calling all others who believe in His Son and love Him. He is calling a few to whom He wants to reveal, in a special way, His final plan for the battle against Satan and his hosts. When He finds such people and reveals His purpose to them, they will make importunate "knocking" their one business and so co-operate with God to bring His Kingdom. Such people will pay a very high price – loneliness, intensity in prayer, ever increasing wrestling, increased attacks from hell – but they are people who will neither rest night nor day nor give God a second's rest, but pray until the Lord appears in the clouds to establish the Kingdom.

Will you pay the price? Will you enroll?

FINALLY, REMEMBER

God wants to know how serious we are. He will not deal with people who are not serious. There are many things that God has for you and for the Church that you will not experience until you trouble and weary Him with your prayers over a sustained period of time. A man or woman who wants God's will to be done at any cost will pray night and day. Such praying is not just simple phrases being thrown at God. It is a matter of life and death, requiring tears, agony, heartache, and wrestling.

Deep praying is expensive, and how sad it is to know that very few believers know anything about it! May we grow up and by our importunity force God to release what would otherwise not have been released. May we develop a holy anger against the devil. May we say to him, "Satan, I am going to deal with you." And may we then, through importunate prayer, war against him.

Some believers pray one or two times or during one or two years, and when they do not see the answer; they are discouraged and say, "God has not answered." If, for example, we are praying for the conversion of a partner or child but go on only for three or four years then place ourselves at ease by saying that God has not answered, we betray our initial commitment for what truly it was – no commitment. If we are serious, we shall pray until the person is converted, even if we have to pray for fifty years.

The Lord ended His teaching on importunity by asking, "Nevertheless when the Son of man comes, will He find faith on earth?" The person with genuine faith believes the promises of God. He believes God and is prepared to importune even when all outward evidence is against him. It takes faith to continue to pray for a husband whose hostility toward the Lord seems to increase with your prayers on his behalf. May God grant us that faith. We need it and must have it. God help us.

CHAPTER 9

Supplication

The Bible says, "*I urge that supplications, prayers, intercessions, and thanksgiving be made for all men*" (1 Timothy 2:1). "*If you will seek God and make supplication to the Almighty, if you are pure and upright, surely then He will rouse Himself for you and reward you with a rightful habitation*" (Job 8:5,6). "*Hear the voice of my supplication as I CRY TO THEE, for help, as I lift up my hands toward Thy most holy sanctuary*" (Psalms 28:2). "*Blessed be the Lord for He has heard the voice of my supplications*" (Psalms 28:6).

Supplication is very intense, pleading heart cry, desperate praying to the Lord in a given situation. Supplication comes when the situation is so desperate that the supplicant realizes that if God did not act, there would be absolute failure and that the failure would be tragic beyond telling! The supplicant knows that no other source of help would do. It must be God and God alone. It is pleading to the one last Hope that there is.

The Bible abounds with examples of men who supplicated. We shall look at a few supplications in the Word.

THE SUPPLICATION OF NEHEMIAH

The Bible says, "*And I asked them concerning the Jews that survived who had escaped exile, and concerning Jerusalem. And they said to me, "The survivors there in the province who escaped exile are in great trouble and shame; the wall of Jerusalem is broken down, and its gates are destroyed by fire.' When I heard these words, I sat down and wept, and mourned for days; and I continued fasting and praying before the God of heaven. And I said, O Lord God of heaven, the great and terrible God who keeps covenant and steadfast love with those who love Him and keep His commandments; let Thy ear be attentive, and Thy eyes open to hear the prayer of Thy servant which I now pray before Thee day and night for the people of Israel Thy servants, confessing the sins of the people of Israel, which we have sinned against Thee. Yea, I and my father's house have sinned. We have acted corruptly against Thee, and have not kept the com-*

mandments, the statutes, and the ordinances which Thou didst command Thy servant Moses. Remember the Word which Thou didst command Thy servant Moses, saying 'If you are unfaithful, I will scatter you among the peoples, but if you return to me and keep my commandments and do them, though your dispersed be under the farthest skies, I will gather them thence and bring them to the place which I have chosen, to make my name dwell there!' They are Thy servants and Thy people, whom Thou hast redeemed by Thy great power and by Thy strong hand. O Lord, let Thy ear be attentive to the prayer of Thy servant, and to the prayer of Thy servants who delight to fear Thy name; and give success to Thy servant today, and grant him mercy in the sight of this man" (Nehemiah 1:2-11).

Here was no ordinary praying. He received the bad news about the condition of his city Jerusalem. He wept and mourned. Yes, people who supplicate have the situation so much at heart that they can weep. He did not only weep. He mourned for many days! It is as if his whole being was breaking. He fasted and then he supplicated. His prayer was peculiar. He was before God night and day. He was so burdened that he would take no rest and would give God no rest at all. He could not have prayed for a short time and given up. How could he give up? The burden of Jerusalem weighed heavily on his whole being. He knew that sin would block access to the Lord so he pleaded for the forgiveness of his sins and the sins of his people. He did not palliate their sin but truly opened up before the Lord in deep confession. He pleaded with God's promises to forgive His people if they repented. Having thus pleaded, he asked that God would grant him mercy before the king.

Nehemiah was going to ask the king for favours which would normally not be granted unless God touched the king's heart in a special way. He, desperate, supplicated with fervour, and how could God turn a deaf ear to such prayer? He answered! Glory be to His Holy name! May we, too, supplicate, knowing that we will not depart unblessed.

THE SUPPLICATION OF HEZEKIAH (1) (2 KINGS 18 :19)

During the reign of King Hezekiah, King Sennacherib, king of Assyria, came up against all the fortified cities of Judah and took them. Hezekiah negotiated for peace and Sennacherib demanded three hundred talents of silver and thirty talents of gold. Hezekiah gave him all the silver that was found in the house of the Lord and in the treasuries of the King's house. Even with that done, the Assyrian king still threatened and mocked Hezekiah and the Lord saying, *"Has any of the gods of the nations ever delivered his land out of the hands of the king of Assyria?"* (2 Kings 19:33). The situation looked desperate and perhaps hopeless.

"When Hezekiah heard it, he rent his clothes, covered himself with sackcloth and went into the house of the Lord" (2 Kings 19:1). He also sent word to prophet Isaiah saying, *"This day is a day of distress, of rebuke, and of disgrace; children have come to the birth, and there is no strength to bring them forth"* (2 Kings 19:3). So you see the conditions that precede supplication – rebuke, disgrace, the rending of clothes, sackcloth, and distress. Unless a man ever felt that he or the cause closest to his heart was in disgrace so that he was in great distress manifested by weeping, et cetera, he would never be able to supplicate. Supplication is the prayer of a desperate person.

What did Hezekiah do under these conditions? He went to the house of the Lord and spread the letter of Sennacherib before the Lord. Then he prayed in the following fashion, *"O Lord the God of Israel, who art enthroned above the cherubim, Thou art the God, Thou alone, of all the kingdoms of the earth; Thou made heaven and earth. Incline Thy ear. O Lord and hear; open Thy eyes, O Lord, and see; and hear the words of Sennacherib, which he has sent to mock the living God. Of a truth, the kings of Assyria have laid waste the nations and their lands, and have cast their gods into the fire; for they were no gods, but the work of men's hands, wood and stone; therefore they were destroyed. So NOW O LORD OUR GOD, SAVE US, I BESEECH THEE from his hand that all the kingdoms of the earth may know that Thou O Lord art God"* (2 Kings 19:14-19). He more or less poured himself to God. He did not use useless phrases. He did not go round and round in circles. He just poured himself as a desperate man, a man in deep trouble, a man without any other source of help except the Lord. He was saying to the Lord, "God if you do not act, I am finished."

When a person in his prayer gets to the point that he knows that unless God acts, he is finished, God will act, for God cannot let such people go unblessed. In the case at hand, the Lord answered the supplicating Hezekiah, saying to him, *"Thus says the Lord concerning the king of Assyria, he shall not come into this city or shoot an arrow there, or come before it with a shield or cast up a siege mound against it. By the way that he came, by the same he shall return and he shall not come into this city, says the Lord. For I will defend this city to save it, form my own sake and for my servant David"* (2 Kings 19:32-34).

God did not only promise to defend the city. He defended it. The Bible says, *"And that night the angel of the Lord went forth, and slew a hundred and eighty-five thousand in the camp of the Assyrians; and when we rose early in the morning, behold, there were all the dead bodies. Then Sennacherib king of Assyria departed, and went home, and dwelt at Nineveh. And as he was worshipping in the house of Nisrock his god, Adrammelech and Sharezer his sons, slew him with the sword, and escaped into the land of Ararat"* (2 Kings 19:35-37).

THE SUPPLICATION OF DANIEL (DANIEL 9)

Daniel was desperate to see God's promise regarding Israel fulfilled. The thing was on his heart. It filled his being. It ate him up. He was caught up with the desire to see God's promise for His people fulfilled. What did he do? He did not only pray; he supplicated. It was a matter of life or death to him. The Word of the Lord says, *"Then I turned my face to the Lord God, SEEKING HIM BY PRAYER AND SUPPLICATIONS WITH FASTING AND SACK-CLOTH AND ASHES. I prayed to the Lord my God and made confession, saying, 'O Lord, the great and terrible God, who keepest covenant and steadfast love with those who love Him and keep His commandments, we have sinned and done wrong and acted wickedly and rebelled, turning aside from Thy commandments and ordinances; we have not listened to Thy servants the prophets, who spoke in Thy name to our kings, our princes, and our fathers, and to all the people of the land. To Thee, O Lord, belongs righteousness, but to us confusion of face, as at this day, to the men of Judah, to the inhabitants of Jerusalem, and to all Israel, Those that are near and those that are far away, in all the lands to which Thou has driven them, because of the treachery they have committed against Thee. To us, O Lord, belongs confusion of face, to our kings, to our princes, and to our fathers, because we have sinned against Thee. To the Lord our God belong mercy and forgiveness; because we have rebelled against Him, and have not obeyed the voice of the Lord our God by following His laws, which He set before us by His servants the prophet. All Israel has transgressed Thy law and turned aside, refusing to obey thy voice. And the curse and oath which are written in the law of Moses the servant of God have been poured out upon us because we have sinned against Him. He has confirmed His words, which He spoke against us and against our rulers who ruled us by bringing upon us a great calamity; for under the whole heave there has not been done the like of what has been done against Jerusalem. As it is written in the law of Moses, all this calamity has come upon us, yet we have not entreated the favour of the Lord our God, turning from our iniquities and giving heed to Thy truth. Therefore the Lord has kept ready the calamity and has brought it upon us for the Lord our God is righteous in all the works which He has done, and we have not obeyed His voice. And now, O Lord our God, who didst bring Thy people out of the land of Egypt with a mighty hand, and hast made Thee a name as at this day, we have sinned, we have done wickedly. O Lord, according to all Thy righteous acts, let Thy anger and Thy wrath turn away from Thy city Jerusalem, Thy Holy hill; because for our sins, and for the iniquities of our fathers, Jerusalem and Thy people have become a byword among all who are round about us.   Now therefore, O our God, hearken to the prayer of Thy servant and to his supplications, and for Thy own sake, O Lord, cause Thy face to shine upon Thy sanctuary which is desolate. O my God, incline Thy ear and hear, open Thy eyes and behold our desolations, and the city which is called by Thy name; for we do not present our supplications before Thee on the ground of our righteousness, but on the ground of Thy great mercy. O Lord, hear; O Lord, forgive; O Lord, give heed and act: delay not, for Thy own sake, O my God, because Thy city and Thy people are called by Thy name"'* (Daniel 9:3-19).

This is a classical example of real supplication. In it Daniel acknowledged the sin of his people with which he fully identified himself constantly saying, "We have sinned .... rebelled," et cetera. The acknowledgement of sin was deep and thorough. Nothing was hidden. There was not the slightest attempt to justify. He acknowledged God's greatness, goodness, love, faithfulness, et cetera, in very clear and unquestionable terms. He pleaded with God! He supplicated!! *"O Lord, O Lord, O our God, O Lord, O my God, O Lord, O Lord, O Lord, O my God" are not he words of a vain repeater of phrases but of a heart burning out in supplication, a heart breaking as it poured itself to God. Another supplicant used the same type of words, "O Lord, O our God, O our God"* (2 Chronicles 20:5-12).

Men comfortably placed, well at ease, can never so pray. Such stirrings and tearing of heart and being before God is the lot of those who, because their eyes are opened, see great issues at stake, should God not intervene.

As we have already shown, no supplicant can go away unrewarded, Of Daniel the Bible says, *"While I was speaking and praying, confessing my sin and the sin of my people Israel, and presenting my supplication before the Lord my God for the holy hill of my God; while I was speaking in prayer, the man Gabriel, whom I had seen in the vision at the first, came to me in swift flight at the time of the evening sacrifice. He came and said to me, 'O Daniel, I have now come out to give you wisdom and understanding...'"*(Daniel 9:20-23).

An answer came for Daniel. The Archangel came very quickly in swift flight. He could not come normally. A supplicant had moved the heart of God in a most far-reaching way, and God, being who He is, acted in a most urgent way. If prayers will bring replies by "ordinary mail" from God, supplications will bring answers by telex. However, telex costs more than ordinary mail!

In our study so far, we have seen people supplicating for causes which, even though they included themselves as individuals, went beyond personal matters. We shall now look at some who supplicated for purely personal matters and see what they did and how God answered them.

THE SUPPLICATION OF HANNAH (1 SAMUEL 1)

Hannah was without a child. Nothing else could comfort her. Although her husband loved her, there was an aching void in her being that needed a child to fill. She went up to Shiloh to pray. The Bible says, *"She was deeply distressed and prayed to the Lord, and wept bitterly"* (1 Samuel 1:10). She was afflicted.

Her need consumed her. She was afflicted without it. She knew only tears, bitter tears, and distress of soul. Such a situation does not give room for light praying. Who would pray lightly in distress of soul?

Hannah was so taken up with her prayers that even Eli could not understand. May be he had never prayed with such intensity. He was an easygoing man who was never desperate, but Hannah was. Hannah describes her prayer in the right terms – the terms of all true supplication: "I have been pouring out my soul before the Lord… I have been speaking out of my great anxiety and vexation."

Supplication is the pouring out of one's soul before the Lord; it is speaking out of great vexation of soul. Very few people know by experience this kind of praying. The Lord Jesus knew it too well. H said, "*'My soul is very sorrowful, even to death, remain here and watch.' And going a little further, He fell on the ground and prayed that if it were possible, the hour might pass from Him.'*" (Mark 14:34-35).

When perishing men begin to touch us deeply and our hearts, souls, and bodies are carried away in deepest identification with them in their lost state, we shall know agony of soul and pour our souls out in prayer before God on their behalf. O God, do this in me.

Hannah's supplication did not go unrewarded. Eli, the priest, said to her, "*Go in peace, and the God of Israel grant your petition which you have made to Him*" (1 Samuel 1:17). She believed Him and so the desire of her heart was granted – she conceived and gave birth to Samuel! God is faithful!!

THE SUPPLICATION OF HEZEKIAH (2) (2 KINGS 20:1-11)

Hezekiah became sick and was at the point of death. The Lord spoke to him through Prophet Isaiah saying, "*Set your house in order for you shall die, you shall not recover*" (2 Kings 20:1). How did he react? Did he prepare to die by beginning to write his will, et cetera. No! He turned his face to the wall, determined to be distracted and sidetracked by no one. He decided to concentrate on the Lord and on Him only. Then he prayed and pleaded with God saying "*Remember now, O Lord, I beseech Thee, how I have walked before Thee in faithfulness and with a whole heart, and have done what is good in Thy sight. And Hezekiah wept bitterly*" (2 Kings 20:3).

He wept. He supplicated. Then he wept and God's heart was moved, for he sent a message to him saying, "*I have heard your prayer, I have seen your tears; behold I will heal you; on the third day you shall go up to he house of the Lord. I will add fifteen years to your life*" (2 Kings

20:5-6). The words of the Lord to Hezekiah are important. The Lord said to him, "I have heard your prayer, I have seen your tears; behold I will heal you." It was not only the prayer that the Lord heard. He also saw the tears. So prayer heard plus tears seen moved God to heal and to add another fifteen years to Hezekiah's life. What if it was prayer but no tears? I do not know. Maybe God would have only healed without adding the fifteen years or maybe He would not have healed at all. All we know is that those tears were important to God. He noticed their presence, and He would have noticed their absence clearly.

When people are completely caught up with God, they are not ashamed to weep. The Lord of Glory did not only weep, He sweated drops of blood.

God was not only prepared to heal Hezekiah and add fifteen years to his life because he supplicated, but He was prepared to perform a very far-reaching miracle – cause the shadow to go back ten steps – as an assurance to him that the promised miracles of his health and lengthened life would take place. God is good. God is wonderful. When He finds the right men, the supplicating men, there is no extent to which He would not go to be a blessing to these men. May we, too, pray in and enter the privileged circle of supplicants. They are God's choicest men.

CHAPTER 10

Intercession

THE NEED OF INTERCESSORS

"And the Word of the Lord came to me; 'Son of man, say to her, you are a land that is not cleansed, or rained upon in the day; they have devoured human lives; they have taken treasure and precious things; they have made many widows in the midst of her. Her priests have done violence to my law and have profaned my holy things; they have made no distinction between the holy and the common, neither have they taught the difference between the unclean and the clean, and they have disregarded my Sabbaths, so that I am profaned among them. Her princes in the midst of her are like wolves tearing the prey, shedding blood, destroying lives to get dishonest gain. And her prophets have daubed for them with whitewash, seeing false visions and divining lies for the, saying, "Thus says the Lord God" when the Lord has no spoken. The people of the land have practice extortion and committed robbery; they have oppressed the poor and needy, and have extorted from the sojourner without redress. And I sought for a man among them who should build up the wall and stand in the gap before me for the land, that I should not destroy it; BUT I FOUND NONE. Therefore I have poured out my indignation upon them; I have consumed them with the fire of my wrath; their way have I requited upon their heads, says the Lord God' "(Ezekiel 22:23-31).

THE APPALLING CONDITION OF THE DAY

In looking at the appalling condition of the day, we must bear in mind that the verdict, as well as the analysis, are God's and not men's. The analysis, being God's, is very accurate, and it portrays a serious situation (Ezekiel 22:23). The land is unholy. It is impure (Ezekiel 22:24). Although it is ripe for judgement, it has not yet been judged (Ezekiel 22:24). The fact that it is not yet judged throws a glimmer of hope. Something can still be done. It is not too late.

THE APPALLING SITUATION IS CAUSED BY DESTRUCTION FROM THREE SOURCES

1. Destruction by spiritual leaders (Ezekiel22:25)

There is a conspiracy of her prophets in the midst thereof. The conspiracy is not publicly discussed and agreed upon, but it is just that no one must take a strong stand against sin, lest it offend church members and the general public, lest it ruin the offering – there is a conspiracy among the prophets, the spiritual leaders. Like a roaring lion they tear the prey. They exploit the people materially and build large, big buildings called "churches" where sinners are patted gently on their backs to hell. They are committed to making money – to higher pay, larger and more luxurious cars and homes, et cetera. The widows and the helpless are not taken care of – the poor are neglected and are not wanted. The hungry are simply told, "Believe on the Lord and thou shall be saved", and eyes are closed to their bleeding practical needs.

2.   Destruction by believers (Ezekiel 22:26).

Believers (priests) have violated (broken) God's law by living in conscious sin. By living in conscious sin, yet going about as if everything were all right, such believers have polluted even spiritual things, for all things that the impure touch become impure. They put no difference between the holy and the profane, the clean and the unclean. As a result of this attitude to sin all becomes blurred.

3.   Destruction by her princes (political leaders) (Ezekiel 22:27).

The political leaders like wolves ravage the prey, shed blood, destroy souls and get dishonest gain. These political leaders only follow the pattern set by corrupt and confused spiritual leaders. It is clearly a fact vindicated by history that when the Church has been holy and vigorous she has forced governments to be right. Poor spiritual conditions in the Church directly or indirectly produce poor political leadership. The Church decides the type of government that any nation has. This is not done by campaigning for one candidate or the other but by preaching and living the high standard of the Gospel of the Lord Jesus. That Gospel, preached and lived, becomes an irresistible mirror and conscience to the political leaders. There are far too many believers today whose preoccupation is the political analysis of the perils of the day, and too few who analyse the spiritual perils of the hour, and yet fewer still are those who are committed to turning the spiritual tide by tears and prayers.

4.   **The real tragedy** (Ezekiel 22:28-29).

The real tragedy is what is done in such times. The prophets daub the people with whitewash. They do this by not insisting on deep repentance (the rich young ruler would have been accepted and given eldership by many a church leader of today!). Then the leaders see false visions of blessing, peace, et cetera, saying, "I feel God's presence in the 'church' today," when God is forced by sin to hid His face. Such leaders divine lies for the people, saying, "Thus says the Lord," when the Lord has not spoke. The problem extends further, for not only are the prophets false but the people themselves have become terrible. They practise extortion (cheating). They commit robbery from God and man. They oppress the poor, the needy, and the sojourner.

These conditions make the nation ripe for judgement - righteous judgement. It is nor possible for God to close His eyes to such a situation indefinitely.

GOD'S LOVE FOR A SIN-RIDDEN NATION

Bad as the situation was, God's love for them made Him unwilling to destroy the nation and the people, THEREFORE :

1.   **God sought for a man AMONG THEM**. It is sad to

know that God had to seek. To put it in human language, God had a need for which He did not easily find an answer. God sought for a man (not for an angel) from amongst them (not from elsewhere).

2. **One who would build up the wall of prayer and holiness.**

3. One who would stand in the gap before him. Standing in the gap before man is one thing, but standing in the gap before God is quite another thing. This demands holiness, the lifting up of HOLY hands.

4. **One who would stand up for the land.**

This standing in the gap is not for personal needs or personal problems, but it is standing FOR THE LAND, FOR THE PEOPLE. **This standing in the gap, before God, for the land or for the people is intercession !**

In intercession, a holy person stands in the gap between God and someone or some place and prevents God from bringing judgement on that place or receives blessings from God for that person or place by effective prayer.

AN EXAMPLE OF AN INTERCESSOR

"So the men turned from there, and went toward Sodom; but Abraham still stood before the Lord. Then Abraham drew near, and said, 'Wilt Thou indeed destroy the righteous with the wicked? Suppose there are fifty righteous within the city; wilt Thou then destroy the place and not spare it for the fifty righteous who are in it? Far be it from Thee to do such a thing, to slay the righteous with the wicked, so that the righteous fare as the wicked! Far be that from Thee! Shall not the Judge of all the earth do right'" And the Lord said, 'If I find at Sodom fifty righteous in the city,

I will spare the whole place for their sake.' Abraham answered, 'Behold, I have taken upon myself to speak to the Lord, I who am but dust and ashes. Suppose five of the fifty righteous are lacking? Wilt Thou destroy the whole city for lack of five?' And He said, 'I will not destroy it if I find forty-five there.' Again he spoke to Him, and said, 'Suppose forty are found there? He answered, 'For the sake of forty I will not do it.' Then he said. 'O let not the Lord be angry and I will speak… Suppose ten are found there.' He answered, for the sake of ten I will not destroy it.' And the Lord went his way WHEN HE HAD FINISHED speaking to Abraham; and Abraham returned to his place" (Genesis 18:23-33).

"*Abraham still stood before the Lord*" (Genesis 18:22). He stood. He was patient. He waited. He was not in a hurry, for no intercessor dares be in a rush. He was holy. He could stand before the Lord without profaning the Lord's holiness. "*Then Abraham drew near*" (Genesis 18:23). He wanted the greatest intimacy with God for he was about to engage himself in a very solemn matter with God. Real intercessors are people who know God – people who, as a result of closest fellowship with God, can truly not only stand in His presence but while standing in His presence can further draw near to Him.

Abraham knew God's heart. The Lord had said, "*I will go down to see whether they have done altogether according to the outcry which has come to me; and if not I will know*" (Genesis 18:21). Abraham knew that this "I will know" meant that things were very serious. Knowing, therefore, how God would act, he decided to intercede. Let me insist with you that great intercessors must know God's heart and, therefore, intercede accordingly. No intercessor dares to beat about the bush. He must know the mind of God.

Abraham then asked God a serious question, "*Wilt Thou indeed destroy the righteous with the wicked? Suppose there are fifty righteous within the city; wilt Thou then destroy the place and not spare it for the fifty righteous who are in it?*" (Genesis 18:23-24). The question was far reaching. He was appealing to God. "Wilt Thou indeed" are the words of appeal. He did not leave it there. He brought the matter down to earth. He asked whether if fifty righteous were found, God would still destroy the place. Such questions get right to the heart of God. They are the product of deepest intimacy! Abraham did not wait for God to answer. He more or less answered for God, for he said, *"Far be it from Thee to do such a thing, to slay the righteous with the wicked, so that the righteous fare as the wicked. Far be that from Thee"* (Genesis 18:25). In some sense, Abraham was giving God a slight rebuke, *"Far be it from Thee to do such a thing." He did not end there. He appealed to God's sense of justice and said, "Shall not the Judge of all the earth do right?"* (Genesis 18:25). How could God not respond to such an appeal? He is more or less compelled to do as the intercessor demands. God replied and said that He would do as Abraham asked. Abraham then pressed further and further. At ten persons Abraham stopped. God did not stop until Abraham stopped. As long as Abraham was prepared to ask, God answered. When Abraham said, "I have asked enough," God said, "Let it be so. Amen." Abraham, and not God, drew the limits. An intercessor, and not God, draws the limits.

My beloved, Sodom and Gomorrah were destroyed because they sinned. This is true. I want to add another fact to it. I want to state clearly that Sodom and Gomorrah were destroyed because Abraham, the intercessor, gave up. He did not press on to the end. Had he pressed on to the very end, God would have granted his request. What if he had asked, "Suppose five are found there?" God would have said, "For the sake of five I will not destroy it." What if he had gone on and asked Him to spare it for the sake of four? Got would have said, "I would not destroy it for the sake of four". He could then have gone down to three and then two and then one. I believe God would have answered in the affirmative. What if he had asked God to spare the place even if no righteous man were found there? What if he had gone ahead and changed the grounds of his pleading with God and based it, not on the presence of righteous people being found in Sodom, but on God's mercy? The results would have been different. Sodom and Gomorrah would have been spared. The intercessor would have come out of this battle a victor and God would have been perfectly satisfied, for He seeks for people who will "force" Him to display His mercy.

THE SAD LACK: I FOUND NONE!!!

"I sought for a man among them who should build up the wall and stand in the gap before me for the land, that I should not destroy it; but I found none" (Ezekiel 22:30). This is most serious. God seems to have gone all over in a search that proved futile. The Bible says, *"Truth is lacking, and he who departs from evil makes himself a prey. The Lord saw it and it displeased Him that there was no man, and wondered that that there was no one to intervene (intercede)"* (Isaiah 59:15-16). God wondered that there was no intercessor! There are only a few things that surprise God; that cause Him to wonder. The principal of these things is the lack of intercessors. God expected that there should be intercessors, but He found none. A few people occasionally pray, but intercessors are rare to find. Men and women who will shut themselves up and pray and pray are indeed rare. My fellow saint, as you read this, how is it with you? Can we say that because of you, the Lord can say, "I found one?"

THE CONSEQUENCE OF THE LACK OF INTERCESSORS

God said, *"But I found none. Therefore I have poured out my indignation upon them; I have consumed them with the fire of my wrath; their way have I requited upon their heads, says the Lord God"* (Ezekiel 22:30-31). God's wrath, though justified, would have been averted had He found one man to stand in the gap. The nation would have been spared had there been just one man to fast and pray.

If God wanted to destroy this nation, would He change His mind because you are an intercessor? May God raise up men and women to intercede, and may He raise them quickly. If not, we shall be done for! Failure to intercede is not a sin against man, but a sin against

God. The prophet Samuel said, *"Moreover as for me, far be it from me that I should sin against the Lord by ceasing to pray for you"* (1 Samuel 12:23). May all the prophets in the Church of the Lord Jesus say likewise. May each redeemed being say with Samuel that they will not sin against the Lord by failing to intercede.

THE INTERCESSOR'S POWER AND AUTHORITY

The Word of the Lord says, *"Let the faithful exult in glory; let them sing for joy on their coaches. Let the high praises of God be in their throats and two-edged swords in their hands, to wreak veangeance on the nations and chastisement on the peoples. TO BIND THEIR KINGS WITH CHAINS AND THEIR nobles with fetters of iron. To execute on them the judgement written! This is the glory for all His faithful ones. Praise the Lord"* (Psalms 149:5-9).

The intercessors can bind kings, presidents, ministers, and decision makers by intercession and bring them down to obey the Lord. The intercessor can decide and determine what bills will be passed, who will be appointed to what, et cetera, at all social and political levels by intercession.

The intercessor can accomplish the impossible on his knees. He can move the hand and the heart of God by prayer and God will in turn get people to act according to His will. Therefore there are *mo limits to the intercessor! The Word of God says, "For though we live in the world, we are not carrying out a worldly war, for the weapons of our warfare are not worldly but have divine power to destroy strongholds. We destroy (by interceding) arguments and every proud obstacle to the knowledge of God and take every thought (even that of the infidel by intercession) captive to obey Christ. Being ready to punish (by intercession) every disobedience, WHEN YOUR OBEDIENCE IS COMPLETE"* (2 Corinthians 10:3-6). The intercessor can smash and bring to zero every thought that is against or indifferent to the Lord. However, to do that, he has to be completely obedient. Only the completely obedient can completely punish the devil. The extent to which an intercessor can bring arguments and all opposition to obedience to Christ is determined by his own obedience. Every intercessor will know some measure of victory over the devil and all the devil's co-workers. However, in order to render men and women totally obedient, in order to have evil spirits obey without question, the intercessor must know implicit obedience to the Lord Jesus.

My dear friend, are you completely obedient in every area of your life? Can the Lord say, "This one's obedience is complete," when talking about you? Can the Enemy say of you, "I cannot succeed to cause him to obey me?" In the life of every intercessor, wherever there is an area of disobedience, power over Satan is lost. Fellow saint, I beg you in the name of the Lord Jesus to take stock of your life and then render to God unquestionable obedience.

The story is told of woman who was called upon by the Lord to fast and pray all Friday nights for five years. Every Friday, she would fast and spend the whole night in the church house praying for the move of God in the city of her nativity. The woman faithfully obeyed every Friday night, and one Friday night, she went to the church building and found that she could not pray any more. Her burden was totally gone and she could not get herself to intercede. Then she remembered that the last Friday made it five years since the Lord called her to pray. She went back home and the following Sunday, an evangelist visited "her" city and revival broke out. She was perfectly obedient and the Lord blessed her fully. May we go and do likewise – hear God's voice and obey Him completely!

THE INTERCESSOR'S HEART

The intercessor must be sold out to God. He must be sold out to the object for which he is interceding. He must love God supremely and he must love the object of intercession supremely. God can bestow this kind of supreme love in the hearts of those who obey Him.

Moses, the great intercessor, said to God, "*Alas, this people have sinned a great sin; they have made for themselves gods of gold. But now, if Thou wilt forgive their sins – and if not, blot me out of Thy book which Thou has written*" (Exodus 32:31-32). He was sold out to the object of intercession. His whole being was involved. The Lord had offered him spiritual greatness, saying, "*I have seen this people, and behold, it is a stiff-necked people. Now therefore let me alone, that my wrath may burn hot against them and I may consume them, but of you I will make a great nation*" (Exodus 32:9-10). Moses said no to all this offer and preferred to intercede. He fasted and interceded. The Word of God says, "*Then I lay prostrate before the Lord as before, forty days and forty nights; I ate neither bread nor drank water, because of all the sin which you had committed in doing what was evil in the sight of the Lord, to provoke Him to anger. For I was afraid of the anger and hot displeasure which the Lord bore against you, so that He was ready to destroy you. But the Lord hearkened to me that time also*" (Deuteronomy 9:18-19). Moses, thus interceding, was prepared to perish eternally (if need be) so that the object of his intercession might be saved eternally. May God raise up such people in the Church today!

The apostle Paul, another intercessor of note, said, "I have great sorrow, and unceasing anguish in my heart. For I could wish that I myself were accursed and cut off from Christ for the sake of my brethren, my kinsmen by race" (Romans 9:2-3). Great sorrow! Unceasing anguish! These are the normal lots of true intercessors. Superficial joy amidst a world at the brink of God's fiercest judgement is unworthy of a believer.

Fellow heir, praying friend; do you know great sorrow? Do you know not only anguish but unceasing anguish? If you do not know these things, maybe you have never enrolled in the school of intercessors with Jesus.

THE ART OF INTERCESSION

"*Upon your walls, O Jerusalem, I have se watchmen; all the day and all the night they shall never be silent. You who put God in remembrance, take no rest and give Him no rest until He establishes Jerusalem and makes it a praise in the earth*" (Isaiah 62:5-7). Intercessors are:

1. Set by God.

2. They wrestle with God.

3. They wrestle with God all day long, not just for short periods.

4. They wrestle with God all night long, not sleepers who worship at the shrine of the god of sleep.

5. They shall never be silent; they go on and on and on.

6. They will take no rest – they are not easily tired. They have insisted with God and received from Him supernatural bodies. The children of Israel and Moses were rendered supernatural. God said, "*I have led you forty years in the wilderness; your clothes have not worn out upon you, and your sandals have not worn off your feet*" (Deuteronomy 39:5). We too can receive from Him bodies rendered supernatural; that are not prone to satisfying the normal desires – food, sleep, et cetera as ordinary men do!

7. They will give God no rest – they will pray and pray and "disturb" God with their prayers so much so that, to put it in human language, God will be compelled to answer them in order to have some "peace."

8. Until God moves and blesses, because the intercessor has clearly defined motives, he will press on until he has received what he wants from the Lord. He dare not stop short of victory. He dare not stop short of pressing on until the answer is received. He must go right on and receive the object of intercession and present it to the Lord as a trophy against the day of reckoning!

Intercessors are also people who remind God of His promises

and, if need be, argue with God until God establishes the desires of their hearts. Moses could plead with God, saying, *"O Lord, why does Thy wrath burn hot against Thy people, whom Thou hast brought our of Egypt with great power and with a might hand? Why should the Egyptians say, "With evil intent did He bring them forth, to slay them in the mountains, and to consume them from the face of the earth? Turn from Thy fierce wrath, and repent of this evil against Thy people. Remember Abraham, Isaac and Israel, Thy servants to whom Thou didst swear by Thine own self, and did sat to them, 'I will multiply your descendants as the stars of heaven, and all this land that I have promised I will give to your descendants and they shall inherit it forever?"* (Exodus 32:11-13). You see, Moses pleaded, "rebuked", et cetera, as he appealed to God on behalf of His people.

Was he successful? Yes, he was! The Bible says, *"And the Lord repented of the evil which He thought to do to His people"* (Exodus 32:14). Moses did not only succeed, he succeeded each time he interceded. On another occasion the Lord said to him, *"How long will these people despise me? And how long will they not believe in me, in spite of all the signs which I have wrought among them? I will strike them with the pestilence and disinherit them, and I will make of you a nation greater and mightier than they"* (Numbers 14:11-12).

Moses, the intercessor, said to God, *"Then, the Egyptians will hear of it, for Thou didst bring up this people in Thy might from among them, and they will tell the inhabitants of this land. They have heard that Thou, O Lord, art in the midst of this people. For Thou, O Lord, art seen face to face, and Thy cloud stands over them and Thou goest before them in a pillar of cloud by day and in a pillar of fire by night. Now if Thou dost kill this people as one man, then the nations who have heard Thy fame will say, 'Because the Lord was not able to bring this people into the land which He swore to give them, therefore He has slain them in the wilderness'. And now, I pray Thee, let the power of the Lord be great as Thou hast promised, saying, "The Lord is slow to anger, and abounding in steadfast love, forgiving iniquity and transgression, but He will by no means clear the guilty, visiting the iniquity of the fathers upon children upon the third and upon the fourth generation.' Pardon the iniquity of this people, I pray*

Thee, according to the greatness of Thy steadfast love, and according as Thou hast forgiven this people from Egypt even until now" (Numbers 14:13-19).

How did God react to such intercession? He granted the request. The Bible says, *"Then the Lord said, 'I have pardoned, according to your word'"* (Numbers 14:20). "I have pardoned ACCORDING TO YOUR WORD" are words of great encouragement to all intercessors and all would be intercessors. "I have pardoned according to your word." Praise the Lord.

THE INTERCESSOR'S COMPANIONS

There is a sense in which an intercessor is a lonely person – a very lonely human being - for, even in a local church that has known the move of the Holy Spirit, there may only be a few who are prepared to truly intercede, for most believers prefer crowds and not lonely circles of intercessors.

However, the intercessor is not alone. He has two sure companions – the Lord of glory and the Blessed Holy Spirit. In talking about the Lord Jesus, the Bible says, *"Consequently, He is able for all time to save those who draw near to God through Him, since He always lives to make intercession for them"* (Hebrews 7:25). The Lord Jesus is enthroned in heaven. He is doing a most vital job. He is ensuring that His work on the cross comes to fulfilment, and what way is opened to Him to accomplish this? That way is the one of intercession. He seems to be living now for the one sole purpose of interceding. It is as if without intercession as a ministry, His present life would be unfulfilled. He intercedes for those for whom He died or else His suffering would be in vain. The Lord Jesus is the intercessor's indispensable partner. Fellow heir, beloved lonely intercessor, you are not alone. Jesus is in the same ministry with you. Rejoice. Rest in Him and learn the art of intercession from Him. Do not feel lonely. Listen, He is talking to you and He says, "You are not alone. You

belong to me. You and I are in the same ministry! Don't be discouraged! Press on."

The Lord Jesus is not the only companion of the intercessor. He
also has for a companion the blessed Holy Spirit. The Bible says, "*Likewise the Spirit helps us in our weakness; for we do not know how to pray
as we ought, but the Spirit himself intercedes for us with sighs too deep for
words. And He who searches the hearts of men knows what is the mind
of the Spirit, because the Spirit intercedes for the saints according to the
will of God*" (Romans 8:26-27). The Holy Spirit intercedes for us.
That is why we have continued faithfully in the Lord in spite of
many pressures.

With such companions, may we press on to the end and receive
the victor's crown.

CHAPTER 11

Fasting

Fasting is the deliberate abstention from food for the purpose of concentrating on deeper fellowship with the Lord and the renewal of spiritual power. If prayer is the rail on which God's locomotive moves, then fasting is the lubricating oil that makes it easier for the train to move on the rails at great speed. Fasting accelerates the movement of the train of God.

There are some things which God will not do unless the prayer of His children is accompanied by fasting. In fasting, the individual feels as if he has done all that is possible and, therefore, God must act in a supernatural way. Examples of fasting people abound in the Word of God. We shall look at some of them.

FASTING AS AN ACT OF REPENTANCE

"*Now on the twenty-fourth day of this month the people of Israel were assembled with fasting and in sackcloth and with earth upon their heads. And the Israelites separated themselves from all foreigners, and stood and confessed their sins and the iniquities of their fathers. And they stood up in their place and read from the book of the law of the Lord their God for a fourth of the day; for another fourth of it, they made confession and worshipped the Lord their God*" (Nehemiah 9:1-3).

"*Gird on sackcloth and lament. O priests, wail O ministers of the altar. Go in, pass the night in sackcloth, O ministers of my God! Because cereal offering and drink offering are withheld from the house of your God. Sanctify a fast, call a solemn assembly. Gather the elders and all the inhabitants of the land to the house of the Lord your God; and cry to the Lord*" (Joel 1:13-14).

"'*Yet even now' says the Lord, 'return to me with all your heart, with fasting, with weeping and mourning; and rend your hearts and not your garments. Return to the Lord, your God, for He is gracious and merciful, slow to anger, and abounding in steadfast love, and repents of evil. Who knows whether He will not turn and repent and leave a blessing behind Him, a cereal offering and a drink offering for the Lord your God? Blow the trumpet in Zion; sanctify a fast; call a solemn assembly; gather the children, even nursing infants. Let the bridegroom leave his room, and the bride her chamber. Between the vestibule and the altar let the priests, the ministers of the altar, weep and say, "Spare Thy people, O Lord, and make not Thy heritage a reproach, a byword among the nations. Why should they say among the peoples, 'Where is their God?'"* (Joel 2:12-17).

So, here we see fasting as an act of mourning – sackcloth, hear-trending, wailing, and crying to the Lord. It is saying to the Lord, "God, I am sorry for my personal sin and failure," or "I am sorry for the sins and failure of my people." Fasting is like saying to God, "Lord, behold my repentance! I hate what I have done. Forgive me." When Israel fought with Benjamin, in one day Israel lost twenty-two thousand men, but the Bible says, "Then all the people of Israel, the whole army, went up and came to Bethel and wept; they sat before the Lord, AND FASTED that day until evening and offered burnt offerings and peace offerings before the Lord" (Judges 20:26). This led to the great victory of Israel against Benjamin.

FASTING FOR SELF-HUMILIATION

Ezra was amongst the Jews that returned from Babylon. The king had allowed him to carry enormous wealth for the construction of the house of the Lord. In his dealing with the King, he had made the king understand that his God was the God of all the earth. Now he was faced with the task of transporting enormous wealth. Should he go back to the king and ask for protection? No. This would weaken his testimony, so he thought. And so he decided that he must have safety, but that it must be by a means that would show God as *able. What then did he do? He himself puts it clearly. "Then I proclaimed a fast there, at the river Ahava, that WE MIGHT HUMBLE OURSELVES BEFORE GOD to seek from Him a straight way for ourselves, our children, and all our goods. For I was ashamed to ask the king for a band of soldiers and horsemen to protect us against the enemy on our way; once we had told the king, "The hand of our God is good upon all that*

seek Him, and the power of His wrath is against all that forsake Him.' SO
WE FASTED AND BESOUGHT OUR GOF FOR THIS and He lis-
tened to our entreaty" (Ezra 8:21-23).

Ezra did not choose the easier way. He did not choose dependence on man. He rather chose the lonely way of depending on
God. He, however, knew that the way of total dependency on God
was a lonely way with a price to pay - fasting and seeking God. But
Ezra knew that that way was ultimately the safer way, for one with
God is a majority and whereas man may fail, God never fails. God
never failed him, for He listened to the entreaty. Yes, God will not
turn a deaf ear to the prayers of His children, especially the prayers
that are soaked in humble fasting. May the Lord help us to so fast
and pray.

FASTING FOR BATTLE
(2 CHRONICLES 20:1–30)

The Moabites and Ammonites and some Meunites came against
Jehoshaphat for battle. The multitude was too great for him and he
feared. In his fear he could have turned to other kings for help, but
the Bible says that he *"set himself to seek the Lord, and proclaimed a*
fast throughout all Judah. And Judah assembled to seek help from the
Lord; from all the cities of Judah they came to seek the Lord" (2 Chronicles 20:3-4). He proclaimed a fast, not only for himself, but for
ALL Judah. He sought the Lord, not alone, but Judah assembled
and people from ALL the cities came to SEEK THE LORD.

As they fasted and sought the Lord, Jehoshaphat said publicly,
"O Lord, God of our fathers, art Thou not God in heaven? Dost Thou
not rule over all the kingdoms of the nations? In Thy hand are power and
might, so that none is able to withstand Thee. Didst Thou not, O our God,
drive out the inhabitants of this land before Thy people Israel, and give it
for ever to the descendants of Abraham Thy friend? And they have dwelt

in it, and have built Thee in it a sanctuary for Thy name, saying. 'If evil comes upon us, the sword, judgment, or pestilence, or famine, we will stand before this house, and before Thee, for Thy name is in this house, and cry to Thee in our affliction, and Thou wilt hear and save!" And now behold, the men of Ammon and Moab and Mount Seir, whom Thou wouldest not let Israel invade when they came from the land of Egypt, and whom they avoided and did not destroy, behold they reward us by coming to drive us out of Thy possession, which Thou hast given us to inherit. O our God, wilt Thou not execute judgment upon them? FOR WE ARE POWERLESS AGAINST THIS GREAT MULTITUDE THAT IS COMING AGAINST US. WE DO NOT KNOW WHAT TO DO, BUT OUR EYES ARE UPON THEE" (2 Chronicles 20:6-12). This is, indeed, a deep prayer, the type of prayer that normally proceeds from a fasting heart.

It was, indeed, the prayer of a fasting man; a man in great difficulty. He said that they were powerless. Only people who are powerless on their own will fast and seek God. He said that they did not know what to do. He had come to the end of himself. Only people who have come to the end of themselves can fast and pray. Those who are strong in the energy of the flesh have no place for fasting, seeking God, and praying. He said though they were powerless and confused their eyes were upon the Lord. That is faith. A fasting, praying man is one who sees a hopeless situation, sees his own powerlessness, but knows that God is able and sets his eyes upon the Lord. In fact the fasting, seeking, praying disciple is confessing human inability and God's ability. May God raise many such in the Church as we see the Day approaching.

As these people sought the Lord, they were in dead earnest. Everyone was involved: their wives, their children and their little ones also stood before the Lord. It was a massive prayer, seeking and fasting action. When one person fasts and prays, the devil is disturbed; when a few saints fast and pray, the whole of hell is shaken; but God waits for the day when the whole Church will fast, seek, and pray, and then all of hell will be brought to naught. May all who lead various segments of the Body of Christ labor and work for the dawn of that day.

The fasting, seeking, praying by a multitude caused the Spirit of the Lord to come upon Jahaziel and then he prophesied. "Fear not and do not be dismayed at this great multitude; for THE BATTLE IS NOT YOURS BUT GOD'S" (2 Chronicles 20:15).

The battle had now changed hands. Before, it was the battle of Jehoshaphat and the people of Judah. Now it was God's battle. What caused the change? FASTING!!! SEEKING!!! PRAYING!!! I want to suggest that fasting, seeking, praying will change the battle facing any individual or group of individuals in the Lord's battle; and when the battle has changed hands, we can relax, for God is able. *"You will not need to fight in this battle; take your position, stand still, and see the victory of the Lord on your behalf"* (2 Chronicles 20:17). And, indeed, they did not need to fight. God fought and the battle was won. The Bible says, *"And when they began to sing and praise, the Lord set an ambush against the men of Ammon, Moab, Mount Seir, who had come against Judah so that they were routed. For the men of Ammon and Moab rose against the inhabitants of Mount Seir destroying them utterly and when they had made an end of the inhabitants of Seir they all helped to destroy one another. When Judah came to the watchtower of the wilderness, they looked towards the multitude; and behold they were dead bodies lying on the ground; none had escaped"* (2 Chronicles 20:22-24). God had won the battle! He can still win battles today if we will pay the price.

FASTING IN PREPARATION TO MEET GOD (1 KINGS 19)

Elijah had stood against Jezebel, Ahab, and the prophets of Baal and triumphed. This was, however, followed by a time of discouragement when he wanted to die. God miraculously fed him and them he went on a forty days fast as he journeyed towards Horeb. His fast prepared him for his fresh encounter with God. At Horeb, he met God afresh, was encouraged by the Lord, and given fresh instructions for ministry. And in the strength received from that encounter, he came again into the battle against godlessness.

We suggest from personal experience that fasting and prayer are helpful in preparing the man of God for a fresh encounter with God or for a fresh infilling with the Spirit of God. During this fast, it is as if we are saying to the Lord, "I need to meet you afresh. My hunger for you is intense enough to cause me to lay aside the normal needs of the body". God always answer such prayers. How can He leave a fasting soul to depart unblessed?

FASTING TO CHANGE GOD'S MIND (JONAH 3,4)

Nineveh was a wicked city whose wickedness had come up before the Lord (Jonah 1:2). God decided to judge Nineveh. In fact, Nineveh was only forty days removed from judgment (Jonah 3:4). What did the people do when the message of their impending doom reached them?

First of all, the people on their own proclaimed a fast. The Bible says, "*And the people of Nineveh believed God; they proclaimed a fast, and put on sackcloth from the greatest of them to the least of them*" (Jonah 3:5). Secondly, the bad news reached the king. He acted. "*He arose from his throne, removed his robe, covered himself with sackcloth, and sat in ashes*" (Jonah 3.6). This was personal humiliation on the part of the king. So the people and the king were involved in the humiliation. He, however, did no leave it there. The Bible says, "*And he made proclamation and published through Nineveh. 'By the decree of the king and his nobles; Let neither man nor beast, herd nor flock, taste anything; let them not feed, or drink water, but let man and beast be co-*

vered with sackcloth, and let them cry mightily to God"* (Jonah 3:7-8).

The king passed a decree. It was an official act. We know that many religious leaders pass their own decrees. The contents of these leave much to be desired. However, it was the king of Nineveh. His decree insisted that there be humiliation, mourning, and fasting by all human beings and all animal in his kingdom. It was a very far-reaching decree - babies, suckling, the sick, et cetera, and all animals were involved. No one was allowed to go away from the decree under the excuse or pretext that he was sick. No baby was too young to be involved. Even animals were fasting! Not only did they not eat, but they did not drink water. Pregnant women and all were involved. This is perhaps the most far-reaching fast in all of history.

But they did not only fast. They were to cry to the Lord, and cry they did, all of them. It must have been very noisy, too noisy for the well-organized, quiet religious corpses of our day! They did not only cry, they were told, "Let everyone turn from his evil way and from the violence which is in his hands "(Jonah 3:8). They repented. They turned from their evil ways -   all of them and no one was allowed to default.

Their humiliation, fasting, and repentance were not purposeless. They had one goal in mind – to plead for mercy. They wanted God to repent and turn from His fierce anger. All humiliation, fasting, repentance must be goal directed. No believer or local assembly dares go about these things without specific goals in mind. The apostle Paul said, *"I do not rum aimlessly, I do not box as one beating the air"* (1 Corinthians 9:26).

How did God react to this fast? The Bible says, *"When God saw what they did, how they turned from their evil way, GOD REPENTED of the evil which He had said He would do to them; AND HE DID NOT DO IT"* (Jonah 3:10).

We know that normally God does not repent. The Bible says, *"God is not man that He should lie, or a son of man, that He should re-*

pent. Has He said, and will He not do it? Or has He spoken, and will He not fulfill it" (Numbers 23:19). However, there are special circumstances like those He faced with the people of Nineveh when a whole nation – man, beast, and all – repented with sackcloth and fasting. Under such circumstances, God, in His limitless mercy allows Himself to be moved by their sackcloth, fasting, tears, and repentance and REPENTS. In thus repenting, God does not show weakness but great strength - the strength of unlimited love and mercy. *"The Lord is not slow about His promise as some count slowness, but is forbearing toward you, not wishing that any should perish, BUT THAT ALL SHOULD REACH REPENTANCE"* (2 Peter 3:9).

The prevailing conditions in the world today are not different from those in Nineveh. There is sin everywhere and people are looking for new ways of committing sin. This generation has outclassed Sodom and Gomorrah in sin, and it is getting accepted. We stand at the brink of God's judgment. It is not the world alone that is ripe for judgment. The Church of the Lord Jesus is everything but healthy – sin abounds, there is lukewarmness all around. Worldliness is the order of the day. Doctrinal confusion, compromise, and indifference are winning the day. God has promised to judge. Must He keep His Word? Can He not be forced to repent?

Where are Church leaders who, like the king of Nineveh, will send out a decree – proclaim sackcloth, fasting, tears, and repentance? Why is it not the normal order even in those systems that claim to be contending for the whole counsel of God? Could it be that those who ought to call for fasting and weeping are themselves caught up as worshippers at the shrine of the "god of food?" Will someone rise to the challenge and help turn the tide? Nineveh was saved. Shall we let our world perish or shall we do something about it?

FASTING TO BREAK SPIRITUAL INTERFERENCE (DANIEL 10:2-15)

When Daniel was reading the prophet Jeremiah, he came to the passage which says, *"For thus said the Lord, when seventy years are completed for Babylon, I will visit you, and I will fulfill to you my promise and bring you back to this place"* (Jeremiah 29:10). Daniel consulted a calendar and saw that the time was up. So he turned his face *"to the Lord God, seeking Him by prayer and supplication with fasting and sackcloth and ashes"* (Daniel 9:3). He prayed, confessing his sins and those of his people. He pleaded with God saying. *"Now therefore, O our God, hearken to the prayer of Thy servant ant to His supplication and for Thy own sake, O Lord, cause Thy face to shine upon Thy sanctuary, which is desolated ..."* (Daniel 9:17-19).

In answer to his fasting and supplication, the angel Gabriel was sent to him to assure him that God would indeed fulfill His promise. Gabriel said, *"O Daniel, I have now come out to give you wisdom and understanding. At the beginning of your supplications a word went forth, and I have come to tell it to you, for you are greatly beloved... Seventy weeks of years are decreed concerning your people and your holy city, to finish the transgression, to put an end to sin, and to atone for iniquity, to bring in everlasting righteousness..."* (Daniel 9:22-24).

However, with the assurance of the fulfillment of God's promise came the prophecy by Gabriel that the city and the sanctuary would be destroyed and his people cut off.

This was bad news for Daniel, and he did not take it lightly. He went on a partial fast for three weeks. The Bible says, *"In those days I, Daniel, was mourning for three weeks. I ate no delicacies, no meat or wine entered my mouth, nor did I anoint myself at all, for the full three weeks"* (Daniel 10:2-3). He wanted to know more about the future of his people. The answer did not come at once. It needed three weeks of fasting to bring the answer through. Why? Because of spiritual interference. The Bible says, *"And behold, a hand touched me and set me trembling on my hands and knees. And he said to me, 'O Daniel, man greatly beloved, give heed to the words that I speak to you, and stand upright, for now I have been sent to you.' While he was speaking this word to me, I stood up trembling. Then he said to me, 'Fear not, Daniel, FOR FROM THE FIRST DAY THAT YOU SET YOUR MIND TO UN- DERSTAND AND HUMBLE YOURSELF BEFORE GOD, YOUR WORDS HAVE BEEN HEARD, AND I HAVE COME BECAUSE OF YOUR WORDS. THE PRINCE OF PERSIA WITHSTOOD ME TWENTY-ONE DAYS; BUT MICHAEL, ONE OF THE CHIEF PRINCES, CAME TO HELP ME, SO I LEFT HIM THERE WITH THE PRINCE OF THE KINGDOM OF PERSIA AND CAME TO MAKE YOU UNDERSTAND WHAT IS TO BEFALL YOUR PEO- PLE IN THE LATTER DAYS"* (Daniel 10:11-14). So we see the is- sues:

1. A mans discovers that God's promise needs to be fulfilled.

2. He fasts and prays.

3. God sends an answer but part of it spells doom for His peo- ple.

4. He goes on a partial fast and prays for three weeks.

5. From the first days of his fasting and prayer, God sends an angel to bring him an answer.

6. The satanic angel (prince of Persia) interferes and prevents the angel from coming to Daniel.

7. The fasting and praying moved God to send Michael to help the angel.

8. Michael takes over the battle with the prince of Persia, and the angel is released to bring the answer to Daniel.

What if Daniel had not fasted and prayed? Well, the answer gi- ven by God from the first day on which Daniel prayed might never have reached him, even though God had given it, or it might have come very late. As we see, the evil spirit called the prince of Persia, was quite a strong spirit. He held God's messenger for twenty-one days, and even when Michael, one of the mighty princes arrived, he could not deal with him at once. He only took over the fight so that the messenger might be free to take the answer to Daniel. So we can conclude that if the reinforcement that was given in answer to fasting and prayer was never sent, no answer would have got to Daniel.

Does this explain why so many prayers, prayed in the will of God are apparently unanswered? God has answered, but the answers are not getting to the right persons because of satanic interference and because there are so few who fast, the reinforcement for final release is absent!

May God open our eyes to see the unseen world! May we be granted a revelation of the unseen powers at work! May God open our eyes to see why some people accept only part of the Word of God, why they obey only partially. There are unseen powers at work. The devil is prepared to hinder. The apostle Paul said, *"We would have come to you, even I Paul, once again but Satan hindered us"* (1Thessalonians 2:18). He again said, *"For a wide door for effective work has opened to me, and there are many adversaries"* (1 Corinthians 16:9).

My prayer is that these truths will burn their way into the hearts of all God's children and transform them into fasting praying people. May the Lord begin this work in me in a new and greater measure.

FASTING AS A MEANS TO BUILD SPIRITUAL RESERVES (LUKE 4:1-14)

After the Lord Jesus was baptized into water and anointed with the Holy Spirit, He was led to the wilderness by the Holy Spirit first of all to fast; secondly, to face and overcome temptation and thirdly to return in power into Galilee for His life's work.

The Holy Spirit first led Jesus into forty days of fasting. The Holy Spirit knew that the Lord needed it if He was to overcome the temptations that would come His way. So the Lord subjected Himself to forty days of fasting. He was not hungry during the forty days *"and when they were ended, he was hungry"* (Luke 4:2). He was hungry and the Enemy thought that he could now assault and defeat Him. One thing that Satan did not know was that the fasting had only made Him stronger spiritually, to overcome him. The body was weaker than it was before the fast, but His spirit was stronger and He defeated the Enemy in three mighty clashes from which hell suffered a terrible defeat. Had Jesus not fasted, we wonder whether the devil would have been defeated so thoroughly and so quickly.

The fasting did not only enable Him to outclass the Enemy in the conflict of ages, it brought Jesus to a new place of spiritual power, for the Bible says, *"And Jesus returned in the power of the Spirit into Galilee"* (Luke 4:14). The fasting, as it were, brought Him into a fresh experience of the power of the Spirit, and He moved in the fullness of that power for the rest of His ministry.

Why are some believers so weak that even before the devil has said two words of temptation, they are already crawling at his feet in surrender? One reason is that such people have refused to appropriate the spiritual power that is so necessary for overcoming temptation. That power comes partly through fasting.

The apostle Paul, at the onset of his spiritual pilgrimage and ministry spent the first days in a fast (Acts 9: 9). Do we, knowing this, wonder why he went further with God than most people and accomplished more than most people in his ministry for the Lord?

Fasting as a ministry to the Lord (Luke 2:36-40) (Acts 13:1-3)

The Bible, talking of Anna the prophetess, says, "She did not depart from the temple, worshipping with fasting and prayer night and day." She spent at least fifty years in the temple, worshipping the Lord night and day. How did she worship? She worshipped by fasting and prayer. She was not fasting to get one thing or the other from God. She was worshipping the Lord by fasting. She did not do it once. She did it all the time – night and day.

And the early Church? In Antioch, the leaders of the Church were MINISTERING TO THE LORD AND FASTING (Acts 13:2). As they ministered with fasting, the Holy Spirit said, "*Set apart for me Barnabas and Saul for the work to which I have called them*" (Acts 13:2). God speaks more to ministering, fasting people. Is that why he has not spoken to you? Is it because you are a lover of food?

Although the Lord spoke to them asking for the separation of Saul and Barnabas, they did not rush to send them off. They further fasted and prayed, and then sent them off. It was a spiritual affair. No wonder the Bible could talk of these two as being sent out by the Holy Spirit.

How are moderns missionaries sent out? Are they sent out with fasting and prayer or are they sent out with gluttonous parties? A careful look at modern missionary zeal, dept, spirituality, commitment, spiritual authority, ambition, and fruit would leave one to think that for most of them, fasting and prayer was not part of their preparation and send-off. The average Christian produced from average missionary effort has hardly any fiber for fasting, as if to seal the proverb that says, "Like father, like son." May God deliver the Church from this! It does not matter whether the missionaries are Africans or whites. One thing is certain, and I say it with humility, too few are students in the school of fasting and prayer.

FASTING AS A FEAST OF JOY, GLADNESS, AND CHEERFULNESS (ZECHARIAH 8:18, 19)

The Bible says, *"And the Word of the Lord of hosts came to me, saying, 'Thus says the Lord of hosts: the fast of the fourth month, and the fast of the fifth, and the fast of the seventh, and the fast of the tenth, shall be to the house of Judah seasons of joy and gladness, and cheerful feasts; therefore, love truth and peace'"* Zachariah 8:18,19).

Fasting should be a time of rejoicing. If we fast to minister to the Lord, should we not rejoice at the privilege of ministering to Him? If we fast as a means of humbling ourselves before Him, ought we not to rejoice at the privilege of renewed and deeper fellowship with Him?

Fasting, therefore, as a feast of joy, gladness, and cheerfulness should be considered normal, for all real fellowship with God is a feast; and who can remain long enough in God's presence without being caught up in the joy and gladness that comes from Him?

THE LORD'S TEACHING ON FASTING

The biggest lesson that the Lord gave to us on the subject of fasting is His example. He fasted for forty days. By that act He sanctified fasting and set it as a ministry to the glory of His Holy name.

He did not only set the example; He taught on fasting. He said that his disciples would fast when He was gone. He is not yet back. Therefore this is the time to fast. He said, *"When you fast"* and not "If you fast" (Matthew 6:16). The Lord expected that His followers would fast as part of their normal walk with Him.

WRONG FASTS (ISAIAH 58)

There is a kind of fast that is not acceptable to the Lord. It is that which the Lord rebuked when He said, *"Behold, in the day of your fast you seek your own pleasure and oppress all your workers. Behold you fast to quarrel and to fight and to hit with wicked fists. Fasting like yours this day will not make your voice to be heard on high… Is not this the fast that I choose: to loose the bonds of wickedness, to undo the thongs of the yoke, to let the oppressed go free, and to break every yoke? Is it not to share your bread with the hungry, and bring the homeless poor into your house; when you see the naked, to cover him, and not to hide yourself from your own flesh"* (Isaiah 58:3-7).

Fasting can never take the place of righteousness. Fasting must be solely unto the Lord. The person fasting should make sure that he is in vital fellowship with the Lord. To harbor unconfessed sin and then to fast is a waste of time, for such fasting cannot satisfy the heart of God. Fasting should not be used to run away from basic practical issues of this life. If there is some work to be done, I must not run away under the pretext that I am fasting! I must be in right relationship with man for my fast to move the heart of God.

Fasting must neither be undertaken for show, nor must it be undertaken to glorify the flesh in one way or the other. Fasting must be for the glory of the Lord and His glory alone. May the Lord lead us into much of the right fasts, and may He deliver us from the wrong ones. Amen.

KINDS OF FASTING

There are three kinds of fasts discernable in the Word. First of all, there is the ABSOLUTE FAST. In the absolute fast, neither food nor water is taken. Nineveh underwent such a fast, so did Moses. This fast (without water) should normally not exceed seventy-two hours.

Secondly, there is the COMPLETE FAST. During a complete fast, one may drink water but nothing else - no milk, no tea, no fruits, just nothing apart from water. This is the normal fast for most believers. This can go on for forty days.

Thirdly, there is the PARTIAL FAST. This is the type that Daniel undertook for three weeks. He says, *"I Daniel was mourning for three weeks. I ate no delicacies; no meat or wine entered my mouth"* (Daniel 10:2). A partial fast could also mean that one takes one light meal a day instead of his normal three meals a day. Partial fasting has the advantage that the fast can go on for weeks, that the person fasting has strength for all normal activities, and that the weakness often associated with complete fasts, which sometimes makes prayer difficult, is absent. The great problem is the discipline required to have one light meal and not a heavy meal that includes the two past ones.

Personally, I encourage all the lovers of Christ to use the three types of fasts regularly so that they are at home with any of them as need dictates.

BEGINNING TO FAST

Every believer should be fasting on a regular basis. In our assembly most believers fast twice a week. One day is the corporate, national fast; the second is a private, personal fast either for self-edification, ministry to the Lord, or victory in one battle or the other.

The problem is how to begin a fast. We recommend that you start on a small scale. Fast for, say, twelve hours and as you get on in that life, you will be able to go on for weeks and perhaps months. At the beginning, your whole system may seem to rebel, and you may feel that if you do not break your fast, your entire being will break. Do not give in. Even acute pangs of hunger may not be real hunger but a psychological response to an in-built love of food in your system. Resist. The more you resist, the easier it will be to overcome next time.

I want to assure you that you will not die from starvation because you have fasted. Prove it by not eating and you will be happier for the experience.

PREPARING FOR A FAST

The primary preparation for a fast is spiritual: prayer. Below are some items to be considered and prayed about with regards to a fast:

1.   Purpose of the fast: Prayerfully sort out with the Lord what the purpose of the fast is. Receive from Him very clear goals which you will pursue in prayer during the fast.

2.   Length of the fast: Prayerfully receive from the Lord when to start the fast and when to stop it. He has promised to guide you and He will surely do so if you ask Him.

3.   Prayer during the fast:

      a. Ask and receive from the Lord a deep burden that needs very deep prayer to discharge.

      b. Ask and receive from the Lord a spirit of perseverance in prayer even when the body does not want to co-operate with the spirit.

4.   Stand victorious in prayer and:

      a. Build spiritual reserves for yourself.

      b. Minister unto the Lord.

      c. Minister to the Body of Christ

      d. Claim the lost into the Kingdom of the Lord Jesus.

5. Receive from the Lord something special from Him to you as you wait on Him.

6. Receive from Him a spirit of rejoicing throughout the fast.

7. Ask the Lord to:

    a. Grant you physical strength throughout the fast.

    b. Take away all desire for food while the fast is on.

    c. Give you the ability to sleep on an empty stomach.

    d. Give you wisdom to break the fast at the end in a way that does not hurt the body.

    e. Enable you to conserve the gains from the fast.

BREAKING A FAST

A long fast, and in fact any fast, should be broken prayerfully and carefully. I suggest the following:

1. Have a special session of thanksgiving and praise to the Lord for the fast. Do not rush to eat without this special prayer time. The temptation to rush on to food will be there but please overcome it.

2. Be careful what you eat. A glass of juice will be the best way to break a fast. Do not follow immediately with heavy food. It will be good to wait for three to four hours and then eat something fluid and soft like light porridge (quaker oats, custard, or the like). You will feel much better if you wait until the next day before you start eating solid food.

3. Do not overeat after a fast. Gluttony is a deadly sin. Use the period after the fast to set new eating patterns that will glorify God and give you a healthier body.

4.   Maintain the spirit of prayer that you developed during the fast for the rest of your walk with God.

THE BIBLICAL BASIS FOR NATIONAL FASTING INTERCESSORS

In our nation, believers fast and pray every Wednesday for all aspects of national life – her leader, her wealth, her spiritual life – and all that pertains to the interests of the Lord Jesus. Although this ministry was by direct revelation from the Lord, it is clearly rooted in the Bible. The Lord said, *"When I shut up the heavens so that there is no rain, or command the locust to devour the land, or send pestilence among my people, if my people who are called by my name humble themselves, and pray and seek my face, and turn form their wicked ways, then I will hear from heaven, and will forgive their sin and heal their land"* (2 Chronicles 7:13-14).

Our nation has sinned. Our nation has been judged. We do not expect that everyone in the nation should at the present time be believers in the Lord Jesus. However, the believers are called by God to humble themselves (with fasting) and seek God's face and repent. We have done this and we are continuing to do it. We will continue until there is forgiveness for all the sinners in our land and until the land is healed of all her spiritual, physical, social, economic, et cetera, maladies. We believe that fasting intercession should become a ministry in all countries where there are believers and where there is still sin and the forces of darkness still prevail.

PROCLAIMING A FAST

We live in dark days. We live at the close of the age. We must have God's visitation in love and blessing or in judgment. It is wonderful when one person fasts and seeks God. However, individual fasting will not do. We must have something else in addition. We must proclaim a fast. We must call the whole Church to fast and pray. In difficult days in the Old Testament, the leaders proclaimed a fast. In fact, there are commands to proclaim a fast. The Bible says, *"Gird on sackcloth and lament O priests, wail, O ministers of the altar. Go in, pass the night in sackcloth, O ministers of my God! Because cereal offering and drink offering are withheld from the house of your God. SANCTIFY A FAST, CALL A SOLEMN ASSEMBLY. GATHER THE ELDERS AND ALL THE INHABITANTS OF THE LAND to the house of the Lord your God; and cry to the Lord"* (Joel 1:13-14). We too, leaders of the Church of the Lord Jesus, are called to do the same.

Fasting should be arranged at the level of local assemblies, towns, districts, provinces, nations, and by God's grace globally. This responsibility rests on spiritual leaders. May the Lord grant them grace to discharge it.

THE DAYS OF IGNORANCE ARE OVER

In the past, little was known about fasting, and so we could go on eating, forgetting that we were living in enemy land. However, now, such days are over. We know what we should do, what we must do. The days of ignorance are over; and God calls all the lovers of food, all the gluttons, to repent, give up the love of food, and commit themselves to fasting and prayer. Will you repent? Will you repent now?

A FINAL WORD

When you fast, you feel that you have done the last thing that you could, that there is nothing more you can do which you have not done. Fasting at the deepest level gives you a claim on God for the supernatural to happen, and it does happen.

CHAPTER 12

Praying with the spirit

PRAYING IN THE SPIRIT

All prayer that begins with God, is communicated to man by the Holy Spirit, who then helps him to utter that prayer to the Lord, is prayer IN THE SPIRIT. It is prayer that has its dimensions and limitation in the Holy Spirit. The Lord Jesus always prayed IN the Spirit. God hears and answers all prayer that is prayed in the Spirit. God is the Author of all true prayer. He communicates to man by His Holy Spirit the thoughts that He would like prayed. Man, the recipient, is helped by the Holy Spirit to pray these thoughts of God back to Him.

We are commanded in the Bible to pray in the Spirit, "*Pray at all times IN THE SPIRIT (Holy Spirit), with all prayer and supplication*" (Ephesians 6:18). "*Pray in the Holy Spirit*" (Jude 20). The Lord Jesus prayed in the Spirit and all the time God heard Him and answered Him.

PRAYING WITH THE SPIRIT

There is an aspect of prayer in the Spirit which is prayer with the spirit. Prayer with the spirit is that aspect of prayer in the Spirit which is the special activity of the human spirit. We can put it this way :

Paying in the Spirit
with the human mind

Praying in the Spirit (Holy Spirit)

Praying in the Spirit
with the human spirit.

The apostle Paul said, *"If I pray in a tongue, my spirit prays but my mind is unfruitful. What am I to do? I will pray with the spirit and I will pray with the mind also..."* (1 Corinthians 14:14-15). Praying with the spirit is praying in a tongue, praying in an unknown language.

THE GENESIS OF PRAYING WITH THE SPIRIT

There is no indication in the Bible that people prayed with the spirit in the Old Testament. It would seem that all the men of God in the Old Testament and in the early part of the New Testament prayed always with their minds. On the day of Pentecost, when the disciples were baptized into the Holy Spirit, they received the gift of speaking with other tongues. Later on, in the house of Cornelius, when the Holy Spirit fell upon them, they had the same manifestation. The Bible says, *"While Peter was still saying this, the Holy Spirit fell on all who heard the Word. And the believers from among the circumcised who came with Peter were amazed, because the gift of the Holy Spirit had been poured out even on the Gentiles. For they heard them speaking in tongues and extolling God"* (Acts 10:44-46). In Ephesus after Paul had rebaptized the new converted disciples of John, he laid hands on them and *"the Holy Spirit came upon them; and they spoke with tongues and prophesied"* (Acts 19:6). Praying with the spirit begins at baptism into the Holy Spirit, for as the Holy Spirit falls upon someone, He normally manifests His coming upon that individual by the person instantaneously receiving the gift of speaking in other tongues.

THE USES OF PRAYING WITH THE SPIRIT

1.   Praying in tongues (with the spirit) is praying to God. The

Bible says, *"For one who speaks in a tongue speaks not to men but to God, but he utters mysteries in the spirit"* (1Corinthians 14:2). True prayer is speaking to God. One can do this by praying in tongues. There are times when our minds are not able to comprehend the mighty thoughts and purposes of God which are mysterious to us. In such circumstances, the Holy Spirit will impart to the human spirit, unknown to the human mind, these mysteries of God. The human spirit will then pray these purposes of God to Him in another language, and God will accomplish them.

2.   Praying with the spirit enables one to build oneself. The Bible says, *"He who speaks in a tongue edifies himself"* (1 Corinthians 14:4). As a person is enabled by the Holy Spirit to pray in another language, he ministers to himself deeply. He is blessed by the outflow of his prayer to the Lord. He may start a prayer session without much joy and freedom, but as that one goes on praying in another language, his spirit will be so ministered to that the joy and inner flow which first escaped him at the beginning of prayer now become the believer's possession. In fact, if someone started praying in tongues and continued therein, he would flow with life. One reason why so many believers are spiritually dry is that they do not take enough time in private to edify themselves by praying with the spirit. The apostle Paul said that he preferred to speak five words with his mind in order to instruct others than ten thousand words in a tongue (1 Corinthians 14:19), but he also said, *"I thank God that I speak in tongues more than you all"* (1 Corinthians 14:18). When was this speaking in tongues that outclassed all the Corinthians? It must have been in his private prayer life. Considering his enormous spiritual responsibilities and his obvious commitment to prayer, he must have spent much time in prayer. There must have come times when he could not continue to

pray with his mind. He, therefore, turned and continued to pray with the spirit. The Holy Spirit then poured out into the spirit of Paul the needs of the churches and his spirit prayed them out in an unknown tongue to the Father. At times this could go on and on for hours. He would find that while he was thus praying with his spirit, his mind remained uninvolved, unfruitful. To avoid the situation where the mind was rendered passive, he prayed both with his mind and with his spirit. He said, *"I will pray with the spirit and I will pray with the mind also"* (1 Corinthians 14:15).

Praying with the spirit refreshes the believer. He gives out himself in prayer to the Lord, and in doing so, he is edified and enabled to continue in prayer for a much longer period than would otherwise be possible.

A PRAYER LANGUAGE

Praying with the spirit is the use of a prayer language that is received from the Lord unlearned. I pray in English and other languages. I have learned these languages, and I use my mind to talk to the Lord about things I understand. God in his graciousness gives another prayer language which I will call "the unknown prayer language." This language in unknown to me but known to Him. It, therefore, enables the one who has received from the Lord the "unknown prayer language" to double his prayer output. The person starts to pray. He uses his mind to bless the Lord, praise, and thank Him. He uses his mind to intercede, supplicate and claim. Then he runs tired and worn out in his mind. The mind is exhausted but the spirit is not. So the praying saint turns to his unknown prayer language and continues his prayer with God. So he is able to switch from the known language to the unknown language, from the mind to the spirit, and with each change, he is brought to a new point where he can continue. It becomes as if he were praying with a prayer partner. When he is tired the partner takes over and prays and so forth. How wonderful this capacity for one person to pray with the force and vigour of two people is! How wonderful this doubling of prayer output by the one person is! How wonderful this partnership in prayer with the Holy Spirit is!

DEPTH IN PRAYING WITH THE SPIRIT

When the Holy Spirit reveals things to our minds that are to become the subjects of prayer, a lot often depends on our minds' capacity to understand. This means that in the use of our mind in prayer, God cannot use us beyond our capacity to understand. This is a very serious limitation, for we know that God's thoughts are not our thoughts and His ways are beyond our understanding. How can God obtain the co-operation of man in prayer about things that are beyond the man's mind to understand? The answer lies in the gift of a prayer language. The deep secrets are God's. The language is God's, yet He works through man by using the human spirit so that man is not left out. In praying in tongues, deep things are prayed through. The Bible calls them *"mysteries in the Spirit"* (1 Corinthians 14:2). Man does not understand these mysteries, yet by praying with the spirit, he fulfils the indispensable role of cooperating with God. This is just wonderful.

WRESTLING WITH THE SPIRIT

Contrary to the erroneous belief of some, praying with the spirit is not just ecstatic utterance, although sometimes this is so.

Quite often, it is battling with the spirit. Sometimes a believer may be facing some severe trial or temptation, or is rushing on a road with an accident ahead. You feel your spirit troubled. You cannot find any reason in your mind for it. You withdraw into your prayer room and suddenly you start praying with the spirit in mighty battles as if faced with the devil himself. You find yourself actually wrestling in a prayer language and groaning and weeping. This may continue for some time. It may be twenty minutes. It may be two hours. Sometimes it could go on for four hours, continuously, as the battle goes on in the unseen world. You are wet with perspiration and you know you are being sustained in the conflict by a supernatural presence. While you continue interceding for the believer in prayer, the Lord moves, frustrates the purposes of the enemy, and the saint is free.

My earnest prayer is that God will raise up many mature saints who are equal to the task of this type of prayer with the spirit. Because of their current shortage, the devil is doing a lot of harm in the unseen world against the Church.

There are occasions when you meet a brother in the Lord and in your spirit you feel that you should pray for him. However, you do not know his need. You are not able to pray intelligently with your mind. What do you do? You turn to the Holy Spirit. He knows the brother's need. He may not want you to know it, but He wants to use you to minister to the brother in his need. So you turn to prayer, and the Holy Spirit leads you into praying with the spirit. He then communicates the brother's need to your spirit but not to your mind, and then you pray it through in an unknown language.

SINGING TO THE LORD WITH THE SPIRIT

We all know how to sing to the Lord with our minds. This is a way of praising the Lord. But to many believers, that is all they know about. Paul was different. We too must be different. He said, "*I will sing with the spirit and I will sing with the mind also*" (1 Corinthians 14:15). We, too, must be different. The Lord loves the songs we sing to Him with our minds. He is waiting for those which we ought to be singing with the spirit to complete our singing. Were are they in your life?

The apostle did not only sing with the spirit. He praised, blessed, and gave thanks with the mind and with the spirit. With his mind he gave thanks to the Lord for the Lord's blessing which he could spell out one after another. However, there were many other things, too many to be numbered, which the Lord had done for him but which he did not exactly know. If he did not give thanks for these, he would pass for an ungrateful person. The only way out is to carry out praise and thanksgiving with the mind for known things and with the spirit for unknown things. This he did. We, too, must do likewise.

IN CONCLUSION

Limitless possibilities are opened to the believer who has received an unknown prayer language from the Lord. I encourage all believers to ask and receive this gift from the Lord. There is no choice about the matter. Does it not matter that you cannot utter mysteries in the spirit to the Lord? Does it not matter that you cannot edify yourself, sing, praise, intercede, et cetera, with the spirit? The apostle Paul said, "*Now I want you all to speak in tongues, but even more to prophesy*" (1 Corinthians 14:5). Let us begin with the gift of tongues that will help us in carrying out the most important duty on earth which is prayer. After that gift, let us go to the gift of prophecy. From personal experience, Paul said, "Now I want you ALL to speak in tongues." That was the apostle's desire. Must his desire for you go in vain? It is also my desire for you. Do not let it go in vain.

To those who have a prayer language, I bring you a word of encouragement. Use the language. Use it night and day. Let it help you to attain impossible heights and depths in prayer. Use it to win victories for God. God has given you the gift so that you may use it. Do not let it lie dormant. Do not bury it. Use it. The more you use it, the more the Lord will lead you into deeper and newer areas of prayer and life in Him. Go on. Fulfil your prayer ministry, and may the Lord bless you.

CHAPTER 13

The local church at prayer - 1

The local church is born in prayer. As people pay the price with God, the Holy Spirit moves and people are born again. As they continue to pray the price, the Holy Spirit brings together born again people and the local church is born. So, from its very beginning, it can categorically be said that there can be no local church without prayer.

It is not enough that the local church is born. If it is to continue as a living organism, it must be daily soaked in prayer by its members. Prayer therefore is a primary activity of the local church. The initial leaders of the church in Jerusalem gave it their topmost priority. They said, *"But we will devote ourselves to prayer and the ministry of the Word"* (Acts 6:4). The apostle Paul wrote his epistles to the churches in the understanding that they were centers of prayer. He did not just write to praying individuals or to praying partners. He saw the whole local assembly as a body of praying people, and he encouraged them to continue in that way. When he asked them to pray for him, he already understood them to be praying for themselves and for others. To the church in Rome he wrote, *"I appeal to you brethren, by our Lord Jesus Christ and by the love of the Spirit, to strive together with me in your prayers to God on my behalf"* (Romans 15:30). They were to strive, first of all, with him that he might be delivered from the unbelievers in Judea; secondly, that his service for Jerusalem might be acceptable to the saints; thirdly, that he might come to them with joy and be refreshed in their company (Romans 15:31-32). To the church in Ephesus he wrote, *"Pray at all times in the Spirit, with all prayer and supplication. To that end keep alert with all perseverance making supplication with all the saints, and also for me, that utterance may be given me in opening my mouth boldly to proclaim the mystery of the Gospel"* (Ephesians 6:18-20). To the Philippians he wrote, *"For I know that through your prayers and the help of the Spirit of Christ Jesus, this will turn out for my deliverance"* (Philippians 1:19). To the believers in Colossae, he wrote, *"Continue steadfastly in prayer, being watchful in it with thanksgiving, and pray for us also, that God may open to us a door for the Word, to declare the mystery of Christ, on account of which I am in prison, that I may make it clear, as I ought to speak*" (Colossians 4:2-4). To the Thessalonians be exhorted, "*Pray constantly*" (1 Thessalonians 5:17). And "*Pray for us, that the Word of the Lord may speed on and triumph, as it did among you and that we may be delivered from wicked and evil men: for not all have faith*" (2 Thessalonians 3:1-2). So we see very clearly that with the exception of the Corinthians, Paul encouraged and invited prayers from all the churches to which he wrote. They were certainly praying assemblies.

Any local assembly that has no vital prayer life has forfeited the reason for its existence and will soon become part of the bride of the anti-Christ, which is an organized religious system that knows not the power of the Lord.

Prayer is warfare. The Lord has led us in the assembly in Yaoundé to give prayer the priority that we know it deserves. We have every week the following prayer meetings: on Wednesday, lunch time, and in the place of lunch, the prayer meeting of the fasting intercessors. On Saturday night, forty to fifty believers pray throughout the night.

The leaders also found it necessary to provide the topics of prayer or to suggest what needed to be prayed for in every meeting of the church. We have come to discover that if our leaders are well prayed for, the training of future leaders also prayed for, the evangelistic activities prayed for, et cetera, the church will move on in God's direction.

Below is an outline of some of the meetings and ministries of the local assembly in Yaoundé. In the pages that follow are suggestions on how to pray for each of these meetings. In chapter 14, we have included prayer requests for each place where a small assembly now exists, being mothered from Yaoundé and places with a handful of disciples, but where no proper local assembly yet exists. The associated ministries - Voice of the Gospel and the Christian Center – are ministries and planned ministries (respectively) that have the whole Body of Christ irrespective of colour, language, tribe, denomination, and nationality, in view.

1. Leadership:

   a. Praying for a spiritual leader.

   b. Praying for the training of spiritual leaders.

2. Evangelism:

   a. Personal evangelism.

   b. Sunday morning evangelism.

   c. Public mass evangelism —stadiums, cultural centers, et cetera.

   d. The ministry of song in evangelism.

3. Growth:

   a. The prayer meeting of the whole church (Friday Evening)

   b. The prayer meeting for the fasting intercessors (Wednesdays) lunch time (in many small groups around the city).

   c. The all-night prayer meeting.

   d. The Sunday afternoon worship and breaking of bread service (in many places around the city).

   e. The teaching ministry to young converts in small groups all over the town on Wednesdays.

   f. The teaching ministry for the whole church in one place on Tuesday evenings.

PRAYING FOR A SPIRITUAL LEADER

It has been said that each group of people deserves the leader(s) that it has. This is because the group determines, directly or indirectly, who its leaders are and what their principal characteristics are.

This is even truer in the spiritual realm. The type of congregation, work, workers, et cetera, will determine what type of leadership it has. The chief way in which this is done is by prayer. A work can pray its leader into great heights of spiritual attainment. Also, by failure to pray or by inadequate and inconsistent praying that work will produce a spiritual tragedy for its leadership.

No work can go beyond the commitment, zeal, spirituality, et cetera, of its leader(s). This means that the primary responsibility in, say, a work of God is that the leader(s) be prayed for. Failure here may prove suicidal.

Many people will like to pray for their leader, but they do not know how to do so. The following is written to help you to begin to come to terms with the responsibility of praying for spiritual leaders.

The suggestions have in mind someone whose leadership is fairly extensive. Some of the needs outlined will not apply to all leaders irrespective of the extent of their leadership. However, we believe that there will be found here material that will be useful in helping us to pray even for a young deacon in the Church of God. It should also help as we ask the Lord to raise forth leaders for His Church.

LEADERSHIP

1. Ask the Lord that the leader should be a man with personal revelation from the lord as to:

    a. The ministry.

    b. The place of the ministry in God's eternal purpose and its relationship to the Body of Christ.

    c. The dimension of the ministry. Is it village, divisional, provincial, national, international? God gives very specific dimensions for each ministry. For a leader to remain in full favour with God, he must know the dimensions of his God-given ministry. It is possible that God may expand what was originally just a local ministry and use it internationally, but each leader must be sure that he is not moved by his own feeling. The command that the Gospel should be preached to the whole world as a witness does not mean that everyone should go everywhere. Each one must receive from the Lord the extent of his ministry and stay within those boundaries.

d. The timing of the ministry. The leader must know God's timing for the ministry. All who are called of the Lord must wait upon Him for His time to begin. God is particular about time. Jesus said, *"Are there not twelve hours in the day? If any one walks in the day, he does not stumble, because he sees the light of this world. But if any one walks in the night, he stumbles, because the light is not in him"* (John 11:9-10). If light is from 6:00 A.M., it means that all that is before 6 A.M. is night – being too early – and all that is after 6 P.M. is night – being too late. The leader must not only know his ministry, he must know when to begin. To move out without waiting for God's time is to court spiritual failure. God only moves with those who move in His timing.

e. The termination of the ministry. There are some ministries that God raises just for a short period of time and then it is over with Him. The ministry may be raised of God to meet a short-term need. It may not have been purposed by Him to last, at least in that form, until the return of Christ. To receive such a ministry and then try to perpetuate it beyond the time of God for it, is to fail. This is not all that the leader should know in this direction. God may, indeed, purpose a particular ministry to continue and yet bring that which is that leader's contribution to it to an end. May he be sensitive to the Lord to know that as far as he is concerned, his part in that ministry is finished. God has terminated it. May he not cling to what God has already brought to an end.

2.   Ask the Lord that the leader will develop an unshakable confidence in the Lord and in His Word. Pray that He will find God's Word totally reliable and absolutely unfailing. May he never doubt the Lord or His Word even for a second.

3.   Ask the Lord to give him an unusual capacity for "spiritual correctness." He should be as infallible as is humanly possible. The Lord should so work in his life that everything he says will be God-backed. He should be so correct that the people he leads instinctively know that to go against him will be to fail. God gives the capacity for "spiritual correctness" in response to believing prayer.

4.   Ask the Lord to grant him spiritual stability. He should not be easily influenced by man and circumstances. Once he has received instructions from the Lord, he must stick to them and obey them whether or not his people support him. Stability comes from spiritual rest. Ask the Lord to grant that the leader may enter and abide in the "rest of God". "*So then there remains a Sabbath rest for the people of God... Le us therefore strive to enter that rest*" (Hebrews 4:9-11).

5.   Ask the Lord to grant him a capacity for clear decisions. He must know what decision to take at the appropriate time. He may consult and discuss with others but at the moment of need, he must know what God wants to decide accordingly.

6.   Ask the Lord to grant him a capacity to inspire confidence. A leader must be followed or else he is no leader. He cannot lead nobody. Ask the Lord that people will want to follow him even where under natural conditions they would rather not do so.

7.   May the Lord give him a great capacity to delegate some of his responsibilities to others. He must never carry the whole weight alone. To delegate, he must have faith in people who

are called and transformed by the Lord. He should see in an increasing way the power of the Lord in transforming and perfecting others who are called alongside with him to serve the Lord. He should of course have "no confidence in the flesh," yet he should completely believe that the Holy Spirit, who indwells and perfects believers, will accomplish that work in others whom God has called to work alongside with him. He must still delegate, even if some to whom he delegated power have abused the delegated power, for angels remain bright even though Lucifer, the foremost of them, fell.

8. Ask the Lord to make him a wise counsellor. Jesus is the wonderful Counsellor. The Holy Spirit is the Counsellor. O that God would transform the leader into a counsellor, standing in the strength of the Wonderful Counsellor.

To accomplish this, ask the Lord to make him a good listener with a few, subjective words.

VISION

The Bible says that people perish when vision is lacking. It also states clearly that the times in spiritual history when vision is lacking are lamentable times! A leader must have vision, and true vision comes from the Lord. Pray that the leader will have a vision that is God-given. It was said of Israel, "*Her prophets obtain no vision from the Lord*" (Lamentation 2:9).

As a man of vision, ask the Lord that:

1. He will see what the Lord sees.

2. He will see only what the Lord sees.

3. He will see as far as the Lord sees.

4. He will see as clearly as the Lord sees.

To see, pray that the Lord will take away from his life anything that is likely to limit or blur his vision. He must certainly see a lost world through the eyes of the Lord of Calvary and see the Church through the eyes of the exalted and enthroned Christ.

BURDEN

If he is to escape the tragedy of being a visionary, vision must lead to burden in him. His burden will primarily be for two classes of the sons of men:

1. The lost for whom he would labour and if need be die for their salvation.

2. The elect for whom he would labour without rest until Christ is fully formed in them.

Ask the Lord that outside of these two burdens, his spirit, soul, and body will reject all other burdens, for they would not be from the Lord. Ask that the Lord will deliver him completely from all the burdens by lost men alienated from God.

KNOWLEDGE

The Lord said, "*My people are destroyed for lack of knowledge*" (Hosea 4:6). The leader must have the knowledge of God or else the people will perish.

1. He must have a deep and personal knowledge of the Lord Jesus in his humiliation, death, burial, resurrection, exaltation, enthronement, and imminent return. Such knowledge is a basic pre-requisite. It must be spiritual knowledge gained through the working of the cross. Ask the Lord to reveal Himself in a personal way to the leader. His leadership hangs on this knowledge, for how can he lead people to a Je-

sus whom he has only heard about but not known? Such knowledge goes far beyond the knowledge of Him experienced at conversion. It is the knowledge of Christ fully formed in the leader by the Holy Christ. Paul wrestled in prayer that this formation might take place in the Galatians (Galatians 4:19). You, too, should wrestle in prayer until Christ is fully formed in the leader. Pray that the leader will not only have spiritual knowledge, ask the Lord to create in him a burning desire for more knowledge of the Lord. Paul desired earnestly *"that I may know Him..."* (Philippians 3:10).

2.   Ask the Lord to grant him knowledge of the Word. He must know the Bible thoroughly. O that the Holy Spirit would teach him! He must learn from man, and there is no excuse for not learning from human teachers who are God's instruments. However, his final and unquestionable source of teaching must be the author of the book, the Holy Spirit. Ask God to do a deep work in his life so that he, too, like Paul, will be able to say, *"For I would have you know, brethren, that the Gospel which was preached by me is not man's Gospel. For I did not receive it from man, nor was taught it, but it came through a revelation of Jesus Christ"* (Galatians 1:11-12). This knowledge of the Word must be both objective (Logos) and subjective (Rhema). Paul prayed that believers would have knowledge of the Word. Pray that your leader would. God is anxious to answer such prayer. If your leader's knowledge of the Word – both objective and subjective – is deficient, you are partly to blame. Pray, pray!

3.   Ask the Lord to give him a true knowledge of himself. He must know himself. This self-knowledge has two aspects to it. First of all, he must know himself as he stands in Christ. He must know himself as united with Christ in His death, burial, resurrection, and enthronement. He must know himself as the person on the throne with Christ. He must know

himself as a person filled with the fullness of Christ, dead to sin and alive to righteousness. He must see himself as able to do anything good and everything that is holy through Christ. So ask the Lord to make him see himself as in Christ and as able through Christ.

Secondly, ask the Lord to reveal to him what he is by nature so that he may never boast. May he know himself in that light as a wretched man, weak and unable. Let him know himself as capable of committing any and all sin outside of God's grace. Ask the Lord to let him know his natural self as the chief of sinners. Such deep knowledge will cause him to want to know another power for deliverance and for work.

4.   Ask the Lord to give him knowledge of the power of the Cross. We must know the Cross as the one answer to the devil, the world, the flesh, and the life. The apostle Paul said, *"But far be it from me to glory except in the cross of our Lord Jesus Christ by which the world has been crucified to me, and I to the world"* (Galatians 6:14). *"I have been crucified with Christ, it is no longer I who live, but Christ who lives in me; the life I now live I live in the Son of God, who loved me and gave himself for me"* (Galatians 2:20). "And those who belong to Christ Jesus have crucified the flesh with all its passions and desires" (Galatians 5:24). He must know the delivering and liberating power of the cross in his life experimentally. Pray that God will grant him to reject all superficial methods that seek to escape the hard demands of the cross.

5.   Ask the Lord to grant him an increasing knowledge of the power of the Holy Spirit resident in him. Paul prayed for the Ephesians that the Lord would grant them to know *"what is the immeasurable greatness of his power in us who believe according to the working of His great might"* (Ephesians 1:19). Claim the full power of the Holy Spirit both in His indwel-

ling and His empowering for service. Ask the Lord that as the leader grows in the experience of the power of the Lord, he will depend less and less on himself and more and more on the Lord, since the Lord said, *"Without me you can do nothing"* (John 15:5). Ask the Lord to open his eyes to the need to be replenished day by day with the power of the Lord.

6.   Ask the Lord to give him knowledge of the tactics of the devil. The Bible says, *"to keep Satan from gaining the advantage over us; for we are not ignorant of his designs"* (2 Corinthians 2:11). A leader must have full knowledge of the devil's tactics. It is a spiritual war, and where he is ignorant of the enemy's tactics, he will suffer loss. Pray for him that he will obey the commands, to *"Be sober, be watchful. Your adversary the devil prowls around like a roaring lion, seeking some one to devour. Resist him"* (1 Peter 5:8-9).

DISCERNMENT

Ask the Lord to give him an unusual capacity for discernment. May he be enabled by the Lord to discern:

a.   the deep from the superficial and be delivered from pursuing the superficial.

b.   the spiritual from the carnal.

c.   the true from the false.

Ask very specifically that God will grant him to discern when God puts an end to a work or when God is leading in new directions so that he may move abreast with the Lord in accomplishing His work.

SEPARATION

A believer is one who is called out, separated from fin, self, and the world and separated unto God. A leader must know this separation in a deeper way.

1. He must be separated from sin. A day must come in his life when he says "goodbye" to sin, enters into the full salvation that Jesus offers, and lives in it. He must thoroughly hate sin in every form. Pray that God will work this in him. Ask the Lord to give him a godlike hatred for sin, for only those who truly hate sin will experience deliverance from it. Pray daily that in his deeds, words, and thoughts the holiness of God will be manifested.

2. He must be separated from self. He ought to know the Cross of Christ experimentally in its capacity to put the self-life to an end. Ask God that selfish interests and desires will be totally unworthy of him, Pray that he will obey the instruction: *"Do you seek great things for yourself? Seek them not"* (Jeremiah 45:5). Ask God to deliver him from the desire to be great for selfish reasons. On the other hand, pray that he will be great for God. Ask that the Lord will give him "God approved ambitions." Ask that he will seek great things FOR THE LORD. Pray that he may be delivered from considering mediocrity as spirituality. Although he must not seek great things for himself, he must seek great things for the Lord, for the Kingdom, for the Church. Pray that, in a sense, he will be restless until he is doing the great things that *God expects of him. The Lord says, "Ask of me and I will make the nations your heritage, and the end of the earth your possession"* (Psalms 2:8)

3. He must be separated from the world. Pray that he will know the power of the Cross to separate him from the world and all that it stands for. Ask the Lord to deliver him from the

love of the world (I John 2:15-17). Ask the Lord to deliver him from worldly thinking, worldly ambitions, worldly peace, satisfaction, and using worldly methods that are by their very nature an abomination to God.

4.   Ask the Lord to deliver him from the pride that comes from success. May he be unmoved, unrelated in the flesh by his success. When the Lord uses him to do great things for Him, may he be unmoved by the applause (or the lack of it) of men. Ask God that he will be "untouched", unspoiled by fame. Pray that in each instance where he has no talk about the things that God has done through his intermediary; it will always be to exalt God. God is able to do this in the life of the leader. God is also committed to accomplishing it. He needs people who will, by their prayer, cooperate with him to accomplish this. Will you be one? Please pray.

A leader must not only know separation from, he must know separation unto. He must be separated unto God. Pray that this will be a matter of fact, of real experience, not just theory. Pray that his separation unto God will be manifested among other things, in the following seven aspects:

1.   Ask that he will have an unusual capacity to be at home in the presence of God.

2.   Ask that his spirit will be totally released so that his fellowship with God would be continuous and deep. Ask that the Lord will enable him to sense every emotion of the Holy Spirit and yield to Him.

3.   Ask that the Lord will grant him a perfectly integrated personality like that of the Lord Jesus. Where there are imbalances in him, ask the Lord to take these away.

4.   Ask the Lord to make him into a man with a well-developed prayer life. He should be able to pray deeply, effectively, prevailingly, and unceasingly.

5.   May the Lord grant, in response to prayer, that he will have a thoroughly balance knowledge of the Word of God and that he will be committed to declaring the whole counsel of God.

6.   May the Lord grant him an unusual capacity to fast like the leaders of old; Moses fasted twice for forty days. Ask the Lord that the leader will emulate these good examples.

7.   Ask the Lord to grant him an ever-growing love and an ever-growing intimacy with the Lord.

HUMILITY

The Bible says, *"Humility goes before honour"* (Proverbs 15:33). *"He leads the humble in what is right, and teaches the humble His way"* (Psalms 25: 9). A leader must know God's way, and God shows His way only to the humble. Pray that the leader will be humble and lowly of heart like the Lord Jesus, who said, *"I am gentle and lowly of heart"* (Matthew 11:29). His humility will be manifested in the following three areas amongst others. Pray that each will be true of the leader.

1.   A capacity to accept negative criticisms without the slightest bitterness.

2.   A capacity to accept corrections with gladness and thanksgiving.

3.   A capacity to accept praise without becoming vain.

Humility comes instinctively to all whose eyes are opened to see the Lord Jesus in His risen glory. Such then put their lives side by side with that of the Lord Jesus and immediately they will fall down before Him as if so say with Peter, *"Depart from me, for I am a sinful man, oh Lord"* (Luke 5:8).

Humility is also a school. Pray that your leader may end in that school, and may he study there increasingly and never seek to graduate from there until Jesus comes!

AUTHORITY

Humility must not be understood to imply the absence of authority. The leader must have spiritual authority derived from his position in Christ and the triumph of the Lord. Pray that he will have authority.

1. With God

Ask the Lord to grant that the leaders of His choice will have authority with Him. This means that they will enter into a relationship with God and stand in a privileged position with Him such that God will grant all their requests. It must be such that when the leader takes up a matter with God, it will be considered as settled, for God will more or less always say yes to him. That authority also means that in the discharge of his leadership responsibilities, he can commit God and God will unfailingly back him. When Elijah invited the prophets of Baal to the contest on Mount Carmel, he committed God (without asking Him) and God did not fail him (1 Kings 18). Before Pharaoh, Moses committed God (without asking Him) and in each instance, God stood by him (Exodus 7,8). This is authority. Each leader needs this authority with God. Pray that the leader will have that authority and that he will exercise it.

2. Over the devil and his co-workers

Pray that his standing with God will be such that Satan and his whole kingdom – wicked spirits, fallen angels, human beings being used by him – will obey him instantly. May he develop into a man about whom evil spirits will testify and say, "*Jesus I know, and... (Leader's name) I know*" (Acts 19:15). They should not only know him, they should fear and tremble before him. In fact his very presence should cause confusion in their entire kingdom. Pray that the prevalent situation where leaders stand important before demons may be brought to an end by the Lord of glory. Please pray. Again, I beseech you to pray.

3. He should have authority over natural forces

When need arose, Joshua, the leader of God's people, manifested authority over natural circumstances. He said, *"Sun, stand thou still at Gibeon, and thou moon in the valley of Aijalon"* (Joshua 10:12). He commanded the sun and the moon. Did they obey? Yes they did. The Bible says, *"And the sun stood still, and stayed, until the nation took vengeance on their enemies"* (Joshua 10:13). Joshua had this authority. I believe that God still wants the leaders He has appointed in His Church to wield the same power in our day. Why is such authority not being manifested today or only manifested very rarely? Part of the answer lies in the lack of consecration and holiness among the leaders. The other part lies in the fact that the bulk of believers have not, by a commitment to praying for the leaders, provided the cooperation with God that is indispensable for such authority to be manifested. May God forgive our sin of failure in prayer for the leaders of the Church.

4. He should have authority over human systems

The Word of God provides that believers, and more so leaders, should, by the weapons of praise, *"wreak vengeance on the nations and chastisement on the people, to bind their kings with chains and their nobles with fetter of iron, to execute on them the judgment written!"* (Psalm 149:7-9). This capacity to wreak vengeance on nations and bind its leaders, which is at the disposal of the leader, makes him to have authority indeed. Pray that God will grant him the ability to use that authority and that he will daily pay the price that is necessary for it to be effective.

COURAGE AND BOLDNESS

Leaders with authority still need courage. This is something almost like high morale but different from high morale in that courage, as something to be found in the Christian leader, is a git from the Lord and not just a natural attribute as is found in worldly leaders. There are a number of circumstances under which the leader must be courageous and keep going. Some of these are:

1.   He must keep pressing on even when all seems to go wrong with the leader's walk with God. There will be attacks on his fellowship with God, but he must keep going on the path the Lord has chosen for him.

2.   He must keep pressing on even when everyone else seems to have failed. There will be Judases who betray, Demases who backslide, all in Asia who fall away, et cetera, but the leader must keep going on. Even when men fail, God is always there. The apostle Paul said, "At my first defence no one took my part; all deserted me. May it not be charged against them! But the Lord stood by me and gave me strength to proclaim the message fully, that all the Gentiles might hear it. So I was rescued from the lion's mouth. The Lord will rescue me from every evil and save me for his heavenly Kingdom. To Him be the glory for ever and ever. Amen (2 Timothy 4:16-18). Pray that the leader will know God's presence in his hours of deepest loneliness and that he too, like Paul, will be able to say, "To Him be the glory for ever and ever."

3.   He must keep pressing on with the Lord and His work when the work is apparently at a standstill and no results are forthcoming. Pray that the leader will see beyond the temporary set-backs. Pray that he may know that even if the work stands still, the Lord never stands still. May he move with the Lord and not just with results. Pray that he will be

taught by The Lord to know that after the night comes the bright morning. Pray that he will learn from the Lord whose own work was as if it were suspended for three days while His Son lay in the grave. Pray that he will not give room to discouragement and despair. Pray that he will rest in the Lord and trust the Lord for the future of the work, which in any case does not belong to the leader but to the Lord. The leader's work may end, but God's work continues. Glory be to His name!

4. He must keep on being courageous and pressing on even when all of hell seems to have been let loose against him and the work, and possibly his body, is relentlessly under attack. Pray that he may not be discouraged but know that the devil may attack but Jesus is Victory.

5. Ask the Lord to grant him courage to continuously and relentlessly resist the evil one's attack on the grounds of the victory of Calvary.

In addition, pray that he will be granted a spirit of boldness in the Lord. The early disciples prayed and said, "…and grant to Thy servants to speak Thy Word with all boldness" (Acts 4:29). The leader will certainly be praying for boldness. May we pray with him and the Lord will hear our prayer, take fear away from his heart, and give him God's boldness. Amen.

LOVE

The leader must love God supremely. We must all pray for him that that will be his normal experience. However, the leader must love people. Pray that the Lord will work out the following in the love life of the leader:

1. That he will be given an increasing capacity to love all the

brethren under his charge irrespective of their spiritual, social, and physical conditions. Ask the Lord to grant him special love for the backsliders and those brethren whose love for the Lord is partial and their commitment superficial.

2. That the Lord will give him an increasing capacity to love, promote the welfare, and pray for those believers who despise him, speak evil of him, and reject his leadership.

3. That the Lord will grant him the unusual capacity to love his enemies, opponents, and persecutors and unceasingly pray for them.

Ask that the love of God will flow unceasingly through him to a love-starved world.

PATIENCE

The supreme leader, the Lord Jesus, was patient. His whole life was one unending act of patience. He never rushed. He was under a deep sense of compulsion manifested in His many "I musts," yet He was constantly in control Pray that the leader will be like the Lord in this respect also. Ask the Lord to so work in his life to produce Christ-likeness so that:

1. He will be patient with unbelievers

They may not receive the Lord after constant witness, but he must never give them up. Some door may be temporally closed to the Gospel, but the leader must always see doors as open. Pray that he will receive a personal message from the Lord that says to him, "I have set before you an open door, which no one is able to shut."

2. He will be patient with believers whose progress is slow

In the Church some will seem to make rapid progress, whereas others would seem not to be making progress at all. Pray that be will be patient with these and pray for them. May he be as patient with them as the Lord was with Peter who, after three years of being a disciple, rebuked the Lord for wanting to go to the Cross and at a difficult moment denied the Lord completely. Yet the Lord was patient with him and prayed form him. Pray that the leader will be like that. John Mark may fail on the first trip, but patience, love and encouragement would transform him into a useful and serviceable man (2 Timothy 4:11).

3. He will be patient with difficult circumstances

There will be trying times of stress inwardly and outwardly. Finances may not be coming. God may seem temporarily to have closed His ears to the leader's demands. Ask God to grant him patience with these and other circumstances for which he has no answer except the knowledge that God is faithful.

4. He will be patient with himself.

He may want to know the whole counsel of God in one night. Ask God that he will be patient as the Lord gradually but certainly works out His full purpose in his life and ministry. Pray that he will be spared carnal self analysis, introspection, and the like, which can only lend the devil raw materials with which to attack.

5. He will be patient when results are slow in coming

Sometimes it may take long before converts are won to the Lord and even longer to see them grow into the likeness of Him. Under such circumstances what must the leader do? Must he abandon the work of the Lord? Must he leave and look for a place where results are easier to produce? No. Pray that the leader will stay where the Lord has put him, and that he will be absolutely faithful and leave all matters of results with the Lord of the harvest. Pray that he will be delivered from the carnal comparison of himself with others, of his work with that of others. Ask the Lord to grant him to be patient in the Lord, dwell in the Lord, and be satisfied in the Lord.

CO-WORKERS

Under normal circumstances, no one who is called will be called upon to serve the Lord alone. Leaders will normally have co-workers. Moses had Aaron, Joshua, the seventy elders, et cetera. Elijah had Elisha and the Lord had the three, the twelve, the seventy, the one hundred and twenty, et cetera.

Pray that the Lord will raise up a team of people to work with him who:

1.   Share the same vision with the leader.
2.   Love the Lord with a like passion as the leader.
3.   Have the same passion and burden for the vision as the leader.
4.   Love the leader deeply and passionately.

Such co-workers will minister to the leader in one or more of the following areas:

1.   By being physically on the field with him.
2.   By serving him in the ministry of prayer on his behalf and that of the ministry day and night, without ceasing.
3.   By ministering to his physical needs out of their material resources, for example the women who ministered in this way unto the Lord (Luke 8:3; Matthew 27:55).

Ask that each co-worker will find his place in the center of God's will and will take his God-given position in the work, seeking only the glory of the Lord and the establishment of the rule of Christ.

HEALTH

The supreme leader, the Lord of glory, was never sick. He enjoyed perfect health. He was involved in no accidents. Sickness is from the wicked one and the Lord conquered him on the Cross. Pray that the Lord will bring the following three things to pass in the life and health of the leader :

1.   He should enter into the covenant of health. The Lord said, *"If you will diligently hearken to the voice of the Lord your God, and do what is right in his eyes, and give heed to His commandments and keep all His statutes, I WILL PUT NONE OF THE DISEASES UPON YOU which I put upon the Egyptians. For I am the Lord your healer"* (Exodus 15:26). Pray that he will be healed of all his diseases and after that enter the covenant of perpetual health and remain in it until Jesus comes.

2.   He should be protected under the blood of the Lord Jesus from all attempts by the wicked one to destroy his life. Satan tried to end Jesus' life prematurely and God enabled Him to be taken to Egypt for safety. Pray that the leader will be safe. Ask the Lord to protect his life from the following moves that Satan can take against him:

a. Death or injury by accidents, poisoning, et cetera.

b. Premature imprisonment or martyrdom before his life's work is finished.

Ask the Lord to give him wisdom to act and avoid the tactics of the devil.

The Lord knew when not to let the people end His life, so He took steps and escaped premature death. The Bible says, *"Then from that day forth they took counsel how to put Him to death. Jesus therefore no longer went about openly among the Jews. But went from there to the country near the wilderness, to a town called Ephraim; and there he stayed with the disciples"* (John 11:53-54).

3.   He should enter into an experience with the Lord in which he has a personal experience of "a foretaste of the power of the age to come", viz, the resurrection from the dead. The apostle Paul said, *"That if possible, I may attain the resurrection from the dead"* (Philippians 3:11). Paul yearned and wished that if that were possible he would so attain it. Is it possible to attain it in our day? I believe that it is possible. May we pray that if it is possible, our leader will be granted to so attain unto the resurrection from the dead. Jesus said about John, *"If it is my will that he remain until I come what is that to you? Follow me"* (John 21:22). This attainment, which is perpetual life in the body until the Lord comes, is the same as the resurrection from the dead.

FINANCES

The supreme leader, the Lord Jesus, was Lord of finances. He owned nothing. He set His heart on acquiring zero million francs. He had no place to lay His head. We must pray that the leader sill have the same attitude to money and wealth in general. Pray for him that the following will take place in his life :

1.   That his savings should be in heaven (Matthew 6:19-20).

2.   That God will deliver him from the love of money and things in every form.

3.   That God will deliver him from dependence on human social security systems. God and God alone should be his Supplier and Guarantor.

4.   That God will provide his material needs (Philippians 4:19).

5.   That God will enable him to be content with abundance as well as with want.

    The apostle Paul said, *"I have learned in whatever state I am, to be content. I know how to be abased, and I know how to abound in any and all circumstances. I have learned the secret of facing plenty and hunger, abundance and want"* (Philippians 4:11-12).

6. Should he have any possessions, he should be imbued with the spirit of owning nothing. The Bible says, *"There is great gain in godliness with contentment: for we brought nothing into the world and it is certain we cannot take anything out of the world; but if we have food and clothing with these we shall be content. But those who desire to be rich fall into temptation, into a snare, into many senseless and hurtful desires that plunge men into ruin and destruction. For the love of money is the root of all evils"* (1 Timothy 6:6-10).

God can work all these in the life of a believer and even more in the life of the leader, but He will only do it in response to believing prayer.

MARRIAGE

1. If he is unmarried, pray that he will only be married if his marriage is necessary for the furtherance of the Kingdom.

2. If he is married, pray that he may live as if he were not married, more so as we see the Day approaching.

3. Pray that his partner will know the same commitment to the Lord and possess the same vision as he.

4. That the Lord will grant them a growing love for each other so that their love will embrace all the lovers of Christ.

5. That God will give them children only if these will come to know the Lord and contribute to the furtherance of the Gospel.

6. That their home will be a center of hospitality.

7. That their house will be the home of a house church.

DISCIPLINE

The Lord was disciplined. The leader must be disciplined and organized. He must be a skilful planner who would not just be moved by passing thoughts. He must stick to the plans that God has given him. He must be disciplined in every area of his life.

Pray that he will be disciplined in all areas of his life including the following:

1. The use of time; he must be prepared to give account of every five minutes of his life to God.

2. Speech; no careless words whatsoever. His words should be few and weighty.

3. His prayer life.

4. His eating habits must please the Lord. He must not be a lover of food.

5. His Bible study life.

6. Every other area of his life.

Praise the Lord who, in response to believing prayer, will accomplish all these and more in the leader he has appointed for His work.

THE LEADER'S RESPONSIBILITY

Those who have understood the implication of leadership would pray for the leaders even when they are not asked to do so. However, it is the leader's responsibility to solicit prayer. The mighty praying apostle solicited prayer on his behalf. He said, "*I appeal to you brethren, by our Lord Jesus Christ and by the love of the Spirit, to strive together with me in your prayers to God on my behalf, that I may be delivered from the unbelievers in Judea, and that my service for Jerusalem may be acceptable to the saints, so that by God's will I may come to you with joy and be refreshed in your company"* (Romans 15:30-32). *"Pray at all times in the Spirit, with all prayer and supplication. To that end keep alert with all perseverance, making supplication for all the saints, AND ALSO FOR ME, that utterance may be given me in opening my mouth boldly to proclaim the mystery of the gospel for which I am an ambassador in chains; that I may declare it boldly, as I ought to speak"* (Ephesians 6:18-20). *"Yes, and I shall rejoice. For I know that through your prayers and the help of the Spirit of Jesus Christ this will turn out for my deliverance, as it is my eager expectation and hope that, I shall not be all ashamed, but that with full courage now as always Christ will be honoured in my body, whether by life or by death"* (Philippines 1:19-20). *"Continue steadfastly in prayer, being watchful in it with thanksgiving, and pray for us also, that God may open to us a door for the word, to declare the mystery of Christ, on account of which I am in prison, that I may make it clear, as I ought to speak"* (Colossians 4:2-4).

PRAYING FOR THE TRAINING OF LEADERS AND MINISTERS

It is important that the Church of the Lord Jesus should have good and effective leaders today. It is also of vital importance that future leaders and ministers of the Church be trained and prepared to take over from the current leaders when the Lord takes them away. The ministry must always be seen as belonging to the Lord. He calls His people to it. He takes them away. He provides new leaders. His work continues even when He changes leaders. The Church must pray and train men today so that tomorrow the right leaders will be available.

THE CHOICE OF FUTURE LEADERS

1. Ask the Lord to reveal to the present leaders those that He has in mind for future leadership in the Church.

2. Ask the Lord to enable the leaders to bear such people especially in their hearts in praying, yearning and praying that the Lord will confirm their call.

3. Ask the Lord to enable the leaders to see the special ministries that the Lord has already given to all would-be leaders and ministers.

4. Pray that any one whose ministry is hidden would have it exposed by the Holy Spirit so that it may be seen and encouraged.

THE TRAINING OF LEADERS

1. Ask the Lord to reveal to His Church the Bible way (His way) of training people for spiritual leadership.

2. Ask the Lord to grant to the leaders the capacity to stick to the Bible way of training leaders and to resist any attempt by the Enemy to seduce them from God's methods to human methods that are an abomination to the Lord.

3. Lord, raise up people of outstanding spirituality, love for you, experience in leadership, and all else that it requires for that urgent task of training others in the spiritual art of leadership.

4. Insist in prayer that the God-given work of training spiritual leaders should be carried out along God's line.

5. Lord, grant that the training be both on the job and aside as your Son trained the twelve disciples.

6. Show clearly the dates you have in mind for the specific times of "withdrawal" for training.

7. Grant all who would attend the leadership courses the willingness and the openness to learn.

8. Lord, guide in the selection of the theme for each leadership course and take your children into deep lessons of spiritual experience and knowledge.

9. Father, grant each one at the leadership courses the humility that is indispensable to learning from you.

10. Make each leadership course a festival of rejoicing at the feet of the Lord Jesus.

MINISTERS

1. Lord, grant that each one in the assembly would receive from you a specific ministry and function in that ministry.

2. Grant to each one the spiritual gifts with which to accomplish the ministry that has been received from you.

3. Grant the leaders the capacity to discern the gifts of people and upon discerning these to:

    a. Encourage them to exercise their gifts.

    b. Create an opportunity for them to exercise the gifts and ministries.

    c. Supervise the exercise of the ministries and gifts and ensure that everything is done to the glory of God and the edification of the Church.

4. Grant that all gifts would be exercised in a spirit of humility and lowliness of heart without any one falling into the trap of the devil with pride.

5. Ask the Lord that the inward cross would be mightily at work as ministries and gifts operate so that Christ would have all the glory.

CHAPTER 14

The local church at prayer - 2

PRAYING FOR THE SUNDAY WORSHIP SERVICE

BEFORE THE MEETING

1. Lord, grant that each believer would take some time alone before You during the week in order to prepare for the service.

2. Lord, enable each one of Your children to get to the meeting-place in time.

3. Lord, grant a spirit of expectancy top Your children as they come to the meeting. May their expectation be to meet You in a new way each time.

DURING THE SERVICE

General

1. Lord, O that your presence and glory would fill the place so much that each believer would be ministered unto as soon as he enters the meeting-place. Lord, may your presence lift off any burdens and take away any loneliness or discouragement.

2. Lord, pour upon the assembly a mighty Spirit of joy, worship, and adoration.

3. Father, grant that there would be a continuous flow of life from each believer throughout the meeting.

4. Lord, grant that the fellowship during the worship service would be such that it provokes an increasing yearning and longing for You.

The Leader

1. Ask the Lord to grant him a good time of preparation during the week in prayer, fasting, and waiting.

2. Pray that the Lord would guide him in preparing the programme.

3. Lord, grant him the spiritual ability to minister life as he leads.

4. Lord, may he be so close to You that your Holy Spirit would control the meeting through his spirit.

5. Lord, lead him in the choice of songs and the person to lead each song so that the singing would minister to You and Your body.

6. Lord, help him to apportion the time rightly to each part of the service.

The Minister of the Word

1. Pray that he will receive a message from the Lord through the Word.

2. Ask the Lord to meet him during his time of preparation and minister to him so that he will come to the people out of the presence of the Lord.

3. Ask that he will be pure and clean so that the thoughts of God will flow through him unhindered and uncontaminated.

4. Ask the Lord to give him the right words and expressions with which to communicate the message so that it will come forth clear and simple to understand.

5. Ask the Lord to guide him so that he will know where to lay the emphasis in his preaching.

6. Ask the Lord to enable him to discharge the whole burden

that the Holy Spirit put on him for that meeting by the time that the message is over.

7.   Ask that the Lord will cleanse him after he has preached, humble him, refill him, and use him in future for His glory.

The Translator

1.   Pray that he will find time to meet the Lord in prayer and meditation before the service.

2.   Ask the Lord to make him into a vessel through which the thoughts of God can flow unhindered and uncontaminated.

3.   Ask the Lord that he will be in the same spirit as the leader and minister of the Word.

4.   Pray that he will be enabled to understand the preacher and communicate his thoughts unhindered in any way.

5.   Ask the Lord to grant to him the exact words that he needs to carry the message across.

6.   Ask the Lord to minister to him as he ministers to others, and that he will go away fulfilled and rejoicing.

Sharing

1.   Ask the Lord to grant to the Body of His Son a Spirit-controlled time of sharing when the saints share the light and revelations that they have received from the Lord during the week from the Word.

2.   Pray that she sharing will be such that it stirs the believers to seek the Lord in an increasing way.

3.   Ask the Lord to discipline each saint to spend time with Him in the Word every day of the week so that there will always be a flow of things to share each time that the opportunity arises.

4.   Ask the Lord for a spirit of openness to share and receive material needs.

Testimonies

1.   Pray for each testimony to result from a desire to glorify the eternal Father and that there will be no room for self-exhibition or self-glorification.

2.   Ask the Lord to touch each one testifying to speak only the truth and all the testimonies will be to the point, Christ-centered, and that the body will be edified through them.

Breaking of Bread

1.   Pray for the Lord's presence to be felt afresh as bread is broken so that there will be no spirit of routine about it at all.

2.   Pray that as each believer touches the bread he will touch the Lord afresh and be satisfied in Him.

3.   Lord, heal any believers who are sick during the breaking of bread, for by Your stripes we were healed.

4.   Lord, grant each believer to partake with a joyful and grateful heart.

5.   Lord, grant Your children a sense of assurance of forgiveness, salvation, and eternal life as they drink the cup.

6.   Father, take away an unforgiving heart from Your children as they touch the cup of the blood of the new covenant.

7.   Lord, open the eyes of all Your children thus assembled to see in a new way the glory of the Lord Jesus crucified, dead, buried, resurrected, ascended, enthroned, and soon coming, and that this seeing will lead to a holy and consecrated walk with You.

AFTER THE SERVICE

1. Lord, may the joy of having been in Your presence accompany your children as they go away from the meeting-place.

2. Lord, forbid it that they should go away from Your presence as they leave the meeting-place.

3. Guard the truths that You taught them so that the wicked one will not come and snatch them before they have taken root in Your children and borne fruit for His coming glory.

4. Lord, as Your children go to live before a watching world, grant that their light will so shine before men that they will see their good works and give glory to Your Holy name.

5. May the products of such lives become members of the local body of believers so that each meeting day, there will be those whom You have just added to be received and loved by the church. Amen.

PRAYING FOR YOUNG CONVERT'S MEETING

WEATHER

1. Lord, grant that the weather conditions be favourable for easy attendance.

ATTENDANCE

1. Lord, grant all young converts to come and enable them to be on time.

2. Lord, take away all the obstacles that the Enemy may put in their way to prevent them from coming, including the following:

a. The lack of funds.

b. The unavailability of taxis on time.

c. Uncooperative husbands.

d. Uncooperative parents.

e. Indiscipline of the young convert.

f. Any other reason, like health, et cetera.

THE LEADER (AND HIS TRANSLATOR)

1.   Lord, grant the leader to love You supremely and to have received the ministry to the young converts from You directly or from the Church, yet confirmed by You.

2.   Lord, grant him to be patient with the young believers as they learn the ABCs of the Gospel.

3.   Lord, grant him an unusual capacity to discern the needs of the young converts, and that he will be prepared to give himself away so that the needs are met.

4.   Lord, grant him the ability to encourage the shy and the timid young converts to open up.

5.   Lord, grant him an unusual capacity to inspire confidence from the young converts so that they will love him, trust him, and open up to him without hesitation.

6.   Lord, grant him to be a mean on whom the ministry to the young converts weighs heavily so that he will spend time bearing the ministry in prayer to the Lord, bearing the young converts to the Lord, and waiting on the Lord to receive from Him what he must give to them and how he must give it.

7.   Lord, grant him an unusual capacity to grasp the fundamental truth of the Word, to be possessed by it, and to communicate it simply and honestly to the young converts.

8.   Ask the Lord to deliver him from a subjective spirit with regards to the truth of the Word, that he should present it without fear and without favour.

9.   Ask the Lord to grant him an honest spirit so that he should be able to share both his successes and his failures with young converts so that they may come to grips with a Christian faith that is real. Ask, also, that he will have the humility to confess what he does not yet know and what he has not yet experienced as he takes the young converts along the road of faith.

10. Lord, grant him the capacity to love the young converts deeply, yet increasingly help them to transfer their absolute confidence from him to the Lord of glory.

11. Lord, grant him wisdom to know when each meeting has served its purpose and therefore must be stopped.

12. Ask the Lord to deliver him from discouragement and replenish him after each meeting.

THE YOUNG CONVERT

1.   Lord, grant to each young convert a great hunger for the Word so that he will look forward to each meeting with joy.

2.   Lord, grant to each young convert a spirit of expectancy week by week, and grant that the spirit of monotony will not envelope him.

3.   Lord, grant each young convert to be open at the meeting, sharing both his joys and frustrations in his walk with the Lord, asking honest questions, and receiving the spiritual help given.

4.   Lord, grant each young convert a spirit of commitment to growth that will enable him to always bring his note book, pen, Bible, et cetera; take down notes; and study them afterwards.

5. Lord, grant each young convert a determination to obey all the truth that You teach him.

6. Lord, grant each young convert a determination to share the love of God and all that they learn with unbelieving relatives, friends, et cetera, and that these too will come to a saving knowledge of the Lord Jesus.

7. Lord, grant each young convert to abide until You come again by receiving the Word taught at the deepest level and allowing it to transform and possess him for God for all time.

MEETING

1. Lord, prevent any distracting noise around that would distract people and disturb concentration on the Word.

2. Lord, grant the practical lay out of the meeting-place to enhance mutual fellowship.

3. Lord, grant the meeting to be joy-filled as You move through the hearts of leader and young converts alike.

4. Ask the Lord to enable some mature believers to attend the meeting regularly in order to pray, encourage, and help the young believers alongside the leader.

5. Lord, grant that there be a spirit of mutual belonging to each other and to You.

HOW TO PRAY FOR AN ALL-NIGHT PRAYER- MEETING

BEFORE THE MEETING

1. Lord, grant each person who will be attending the prayer-meeting to prepare for the meeting throughout the week by walking in purity and power before the Lord so that the meeting will not be hindered by sin in any way.

2. Lord, grant all who are coming to the meeting to prepare for it that day by:

    a. Taking time before Lord in pre-meeting fellowship.

    b. Taking time during the day to fully rest in the body and sleep.

3. Lord, grant weather conditions that will enhance attendance of the meeting in good physical conditions – unsoaked by rain, unwashed in mud, et cetera.

4. Lord, prepare and bring to the meeting all who have been set apart by You for the ministry of prayer all night long.

AT THE MEETING

1. Lord, grant a spirit of prayer to each person who is at the meeting.

2. Lord, grant a special burden of prayer to each person at the meeting, a burden big enough to drive away every hindrance.

3. Lord, grant each person present to be physically alert by:

    a. Taking away all tiredness.

    b. Taking away all laziness and idleness

    c. Taking away all forms of physical distractions, e.g., too much heat/cold; excessive noise; unpleasant body odours; and sleep.

4.   Lord, grant each person present to be spiritually alert by:

a. Taking away all frustrations encountered during the day that may weigh on the spirit.

b. Taking away all discouragement.

c. Liberating each spirit present.

d. Taking way any depressive moods that could cause some to withdraw.

e. Taking away any spirit of loneliness that could make some to feel left out.

f. Granting to each child of Yours a capacity to guard his spirit from all forms of outward and inward distractions.

5.   Lord, grant each prayer offered to be:

a. Powerful.

b. With few words that flow from the heart and not just from the head.

c. Deep, capable of reaching out to the Spirit of God.

d. Fervent.

e. Broad, including all that God would include.

f. Edifying to other prayer partners.

g. Victorious.

h. Cohering, not scattered and disorganized.

6.   Lord, grant each "watchman" to press through the night (in prayer and watching) and not give in to slumber or tiredness before it is morning.

7.   Lord, grant all who are praying to press through as a Body until the prayer night is over.

THE BREAK TIME

1. Lord, control and guide as to when the break should be taken.

2. Lord, control what is shared during the break, enabling it to be:

    a. Glorifying to the Lord.

    b. Edifying to the believer.

    c. The result of a person giving himself away.

3. Lord, grant the break to refresh the "watchmen" and renew their strength and capacity for alertness.

THE SINGING

1. Lord, control when each song is to come in so that it may come in to enhance the spirit of prayer and not to interfere with it.

2. Lord, control the choice of songs so that no song may be sung that would cause spiritual disharmony.

3. Lord, control who gives what song so that the tuning and the leading in song would result from and reflect the different ministries in song.

4. Lord, grant that the singing should:

    a. Glorify the Lord.

    b. Edify the saints.

    c. Be joyful.

    d. Be full of praise.

    e. Avoid the shouting that disturbs the neighbours and distracts the spirit from prayer.

FELLOWSHIP

1. Lord, grant a deep spirit of fellowship during the night of prayer by granting:

    a. A spirit of unity in purpose.

    b. Openness to each other.

    c. An increased love each for the other.

2. Lord, grant the ministry of praying for each other to be deep and caring.

3. Lord, grant a spirit of honesty so that the testimonies will be rooted in truth and spoken in truth.

4. Lord, grant the needs of the "watchmen" as they present them to You during the night of prayer.

THE LEADER

1. Lord, grant him to prepare for the meeting before You on his knees.

2. Lord, grant him to receive from You the topics to be prayed through that night.

3. Lord, give him a special word of exhortation from You for the brethren that would be specially suited to the needs of that night.

4. Lord, grant him the special capacity to control the spirits of all the people present and to lead all of them in prayer.

5. Lord, grant him to sense the direction in which the Holy Spirit is leading the meeting and to follow it, taking every one along with him.

6. Lord, give him the special capacity to draw in the shy, the timid, the withdrawn, et cetera, to pray and find joy in so doing.

7.   Lord, fill him with joy and renewed purpose as he leads your people in prayer and watching.

FINALLY

1.   Lord, grant the time of stopping the meeting to be dictated by the Holy Spirit.

2.   Lord, grant the leader to be able to sense the time when the Holy Spirit has brought the meeting to and end and not close it before that time or drag on long after that time.

3.   Lord, grant each "watchman" to feel a sense of fulfilment as the meeting comes to an end and a joy that he has been involved in the crucial business of the Kingdom.

4.   Lord, grant each one to leave with a spirit of satisfaction that will enable him to begin to look forward to and prepare for the next prayer night.

5.   Lord, provide transport for each one and grant journeying mercies as your children travel to their different homes.

6.   Lord, grant the extra spiritual overflow from the prayer night to bless each assembly where the "watchmen" go to fellowship that Sunday morning.

7.   Lord, be exalted, glorified, and praised for this whole ministry.

PERSONAL EVANGELISM

THE ONE TO EVANGELIZE

The Need

1.   Lord, grant to each believer full knowledge of the fact that the one reason why You did not take him to heaven imme-

diately when he believed was that he may become one who makes disciples for Jesus of all men. Grant him to truly know that that is the one reason for his life as a believer on earth.

2.   Lord, convert this knowledge into a burden so that with Paul he too can say from the heart, "Constraint is laid on me, woe unto me if I preach not the Gospel."

3.   Lord, remind him of the fact that if he did not witness and sinners died in their sin, their blood would be upon him and he would answer for it.

4.   Lord, grant him special love and compassion for those who do not know You so that his love and compassion will compel him to do everything and anything to bring them to the Lord Jesus.

5.   A. May the responsibility, compassion, and love enable him to press on at any cost, paying the full price and refusing to yield to discouragement.

B. May he see himself as a dying man before a dying world and therefore know the urgency of the task.

The Qualification

1.   Lord, grant each believer to walk close to You so that You can draw others to Yourself through him. Grant him to be consecrated and separated from sin in every way.

2.   Lord, grant the life of Christ to be visible in that of the believer, that his character may be Christ-like so that his life does not contradict his message.

3.   Lord, grant the believer to be baptized into the Holy Spirit and be filled continuously by the Holy Spirit so that his ministry will be in power.

4.   Lord, grant the believer a personal revelation of the Holy

Spirit and be filled continuously to bear witness side by side with him to the Lord Jesus.

5.   Lord, grant the believer to know You as the Lord of all authority who is totally in control and who will ensure that His purpose to save sinners is accomplished.

6.   Lord, grant revelation knowledge of the Lord Jesus as the only Way, the only Truth, and the only Life to be the witness's possession and that this knowledge will help him to labour among all, even religious people who do not know the ONLY WAY.

7.   Lord, grant the witness to know You as the One who has sent him and therefore be assured of Your full backing and therefore witness with all authority.

8.   Lord, grant the witness to know that the Gospel is the POWER OF GOD UNTO SALVATION to every one who believes and as such its failure is impossible.

9.   Lord, grant each witness to know the Word of God as settled forever in heaven and therefore have absolute faith in it.

10. Lord, grant the witness a thorough knowledge of Scripture as a whole and a special knowledge of those aspects of Scripture that pertain to communicating the Gospel.

11. Lord, enable him to use the Word as the Sword of God in the ministry and battle for souls.

12. Lord, grant the witness a special sensitivity to the Holy Spirit's leading and an unequalled commitment to obeying His leading as he goes out to reach out to those who are outside the Lord Jesus. Grant that in this wise he will detect prepared hearts from all the others who are not yet ready to listen.

THE ENCOUNTER BETWEEN THE SAINT AND THE SINNER

1. Lord, grant the witness to know the one before him as a lost sinner on his way to hell unless God does something for him.

2. Lord, open the eyes of the witness to see that he is in spiritual warfare and therefore must use his authority in Christ to loose this person from spiritual blindness, deafness, and bondage in one form or the other.

3. Lord, grant the saint to be polite, courteous, and tactful as he approaches the unbeliever.

4. Father, grant the witness the appropriate opening words that will draw the attention of the unbeliever and place him at ease in his presence.

5. Lord, grant the unbeliever confidence in the believer so that be will speak out his mind without pretence or hypocrisy and a proper dialogue can be established between the two.

6. Lord, create an atmosphere that is relaxed, personal, and serious, and take away any tendencies towards uncalled for frivolity and light-heartedness.

7. Father, grant the believer to know the spirit of the unbeliever, discerning and understanding, the unbeliever's spoken and unspoken thoughts and assessing his true condition.

8. Lord, may the witness be patient, listen carefully, sympathize, and yet be sharp as need arises.

9. Grant Your child, O Lord, the particular approach to the presentation of the Gospel the right Bible references, and the right illustrations that the particular sinner needs.

10. Lord, may Your authority rest so powerfully on Your servant that he will speak like "God" to the unbeliever.

11. Lord, grant the saint openness towards the unbeliever and stark honesty, especially as he shares his testimony with the

unbeliever. Forbid, Lord, that he should lie to "help" You.

12.   Father, by Your Spirit, keep the discussion on the central is-sue of Jesus and how to know Him and put to flight every attempt of the Enemy to cause them to drift to secondary issues.

13.   Lord, if the need arises, grant the believer the confidence and assurance to lay hands on the unbeliever and heal him in the name of the Lord and deliver him from any demons which reside in him.

14.   Father, enable Your servant to know when there is genuine conviction of sin and revelation of the Lord Jesus and so lead the unbeliever into repentance towards God and faith in the Lord Jesus.

15.   As the person receives Your Son, Father grant him assurance of pardon and eternal live.

16.   Enable the young convert to be shown a meeting where the life of the Lord Jesus takes place.

AFTER THAT PARTICULAR OUTREACH SESSION

1.   Lord, may Your servant return with joy and thanksgiving to You for having ministered in Your name.

2.   Fill him afresh with Your power and love so that he may continue to minister life.

3.   Lord. , may he establish a prayer list with comments from that outreach.

4.   May he pray fervently for those who showed no interest in the Gospel.

5.   Lord, place a special burden on his heart for those who heard the Word, were touched, but had not yet come to the place of commitment. Enable him to visit such, O Lord, or write to them, praying and pleading with You until You save them.

6.   Lord, enable him to keep all the promises that he made to any such persons.

7.   Lord, enable him to visit the young convert in the next few days, pray with him, teach him how to have a quiet time, introduce him to other believers, and bring him to a living assembly.

8.   Lord, enable him to continue to pray for, and minister to the young convert until he is baptized in water, baptized into the Holy Spirit, separated from the world, and growing up into maturity in the Lord.

When No One Believes

1.   Lord, encourage Your child when his efforts do not seem to bear immediate results so that the wicked one may not attack him with discouragement and so side-track him.

2.   Father, do not allow any active witnesses unto Your Son to go for extended periods of real witnessing without any visible fruit, unless it be to teach them some special lesson.

3.   Lord, may the fruit abide and so satisfy Your heart.

PRAYING FOR THE MINISTRY OF SONG (HIS AMBASSADORS AND LES SEMEURS)

PREPARATION (PRACTICE)

1.   Lord, grant each person in the ministry to be called into it personally and by You.

2.   Lord, grant them an overriding purpose for the ministry, which will leave no room for any other purpose.

3.   Lord, take away any desire to sing for fleshly reasons, like

self-display, human applause, et cetera.

4. Lord, provide good weather for the practice days.

5. Lord, grant each one going to the practice meeting to find transport easily and on time.

6. Lord, grant each singer to be able to get there on time so that the other singers are not kept waiting.

7. Lord, unite all of them, giving them the same mind and the same thoughts, so that the Enemy will have no opportunity to interfere.

8. Lord, weld them into a team of lovers who love You and love each other dearly.

9. Lord, grant them Your intelligence so that they will learn the songs quickly and retain the words easily.

10. Lord, grant each practice session to be a festival of rejoicing and blessing so that they will look forward to them with spiritual eagerness.

11. Lord, enable each practice session to be preceded and followed by deep prayer at a personal level.

12. Lord, protect the musical instruments under the blood of the Lamb and grant special ability to those playing the instruments so that they will continue to improve on their techniques and their performance.

13. Lord, raise up more people and grant other instruments so that the volume and quality of praise by instruments that comes to You will increase.

14. Lord, lead them by Your gentle Spirit in the choice of songs to be prepared for the following performance and grant them unity about the songs.

15. Lord, grant them a spirit of mutual submission each to the other and to the leaders who have been placed by the Church to direct them.

THE PERFORMANCE

1. Lord, may the entire performance be in the power of the Holy Spirit for the glory of Christ.

2. Lord, may their voices be at their best and may the words come out with such clarity that the audience will understand the meaning of the songs.

3. Lord, may the message of the songs carry in itself converting and transforming power.

4. Lord, may the physical appearance of the singers and their whole stage posture testify to the God who saw everything that he had made and it was "very good."

5. Lord, liberate each singer completely (body, soul, and spirit) so that they will give themselves away as they sing.

6. Lord, grant the audience to understand the words of the songs and not be carried away with just the melody of the songs.

7. Lord, keep Your ministers humble so that they will not be carried away carnally by the applause of men.

8. Lord, keep the whole performance protected under the blood of Jesus so that the Enemy will have no access to it whatsoever.

9. Lord, grant the ministry to be in such power of the Holy Spirit so that as men listen they will be convinced and turn to the Lord Jesus.

Praying for the Tuesday Teaching Ministry

EXTERNAL FACTORS

1. Lord, grant excellent weather for the meeting – weather that will enhance the success of the meeting.
2. Ask the Lord to provide transportation for the saints as they come to the meeting so that all will be there at 5:15 P.M.
3. Lord, provide taxi money to those who cannot afford it.
4. Lord, take away all the attempts of the devil to give believers excuses for lateness.

ATTENDANCE

1. Lord, enable all believers to come to be taught.
2. Destroy all the works of Satan that aim at keeping believers away - visitors, oppression from parents and husbands, timetables, poor health, indiscipline, et cetera.

PRE-MEETING PREPARATION

1. Ask the Lord to give each believer some time before Him for personal preparation before the meeting.
2. Ask the Lord to convict all believers of any sin in their lives so that they will confess it and be cleansed before coming.
3. Lord, enable each believer to discharge his burdens before you: burdens of tiredness, weariness, purposelessness, anxiety, frustration, et cetera.
4. Fill every believer afresh with the Holy Spirit so that each believer will come to the meeting fresh and in good spiritual health.

5.   Lord, grant to each one who is coming to the meeting a deep spirit of expectancy that You will speak clearly.

6.   Grant each one spiritual receptivity, understanding, retention, and obedience.

ON ARRIVAL

1.   Lord, guide each believer to the place where You want him to sit in order to exert and/or receive the right spiritual influence.

2.   Lord, grant a calm prayerful spirit to Your children as they come in place of a noisy, undisciplined spirit.

3.   Enable life to flow unconsciously from each saint to those immediately around him.

THE LEADER (AND HIS TRANSLATOR)

1.   Lord, grant them to be channels of blessings for the Body of Christ.

2.   Lord, guide them in the preparation of the programme so that all that the Lord wants included will be in it.

3.   Lord, guide them in the right distribution of time to each part of the programme.

4.   Lord, guide them in the choice of songs and on who should lead what song.

5.   Lord, may Your life so fill them that there will be a spiritual flow during the whole meeting.

6.   Grant them a spirit of rejoicing that will spread out to the whole assembly.

7.   Father, refill them and give them humility so that they can be used again.

THE TEACHER

1. Lord, grant that before he comes to meet men, he should first of all have met You.

2. Lord, grant him to have taken time to be taught by You and led into obedience before he comes to teach others.

3. Lord, make him pure and spotless so that Your thoughts will flow unhindered and unsullied.

4. Lord, grant him a very special anointing with the Holy Spirit for the ministry that evening.

5. Lord, may his thoughts come out in clarity and may You enable him to make the message clear and simple.

6. Lord, unite him – spirit, soul, and body – to Yourself, to the translator, and to the audience so that the ministry will have maximum effect.

7. Lord, enable him to stress what must be stressed and pass by what is trivial.

8. Lord, may his appearance, posture, gestures, and all help to advance Your Kingdom.

9. Lord, fill him with joy as he serves You.

10. Replenish him as he serves You so that he may not grow dry.

11. Lord, humble him as You use him so that he may not be taken in by the sin of pride and fall into Your judgment.

12. May You receive all the glory from the ministry as You enable Christ to be seen in the teacher.

THE TRANSLATOR

1. Lord, may he meet You in secret before coming to meet men in public.

2. Lord, may he be pure and spotless so that Your thoughts will flow through him uninhibited and unsullied.

3.   Lord, make his thoughts come out clearly and simply so as to be easily understood.

4.   Lord, anoint him with the Holy Spirit in a very special way for that evening.

5.   Lord, unite him – spirit, soul, and body – to Yourself, to the teacher, and to the audience, so that in harmony the ministry may produce maximum impact for the Lord.

6.   Lord, give him an unusual capacity to understand the teacher.

7.   Lord, grant him the special words, phrases, and expressions that he needs to communicate that which the Holy Spirit is saying through the teacher.

8.   Enable him to communicate life and to flow out to the audience.

9.   Lord, may his total person – looks, appearance, clothing, gestures – proclaim Christ crucified and risen.

10. Lord, may he know the joy of being used by You, but may he be delivered from pride.

11. Fill him after use and prepare him for further ministry.

PRAYING FOR A YOUNG ASSEMBLY IN A NEW AREA OF WORK

BINDING THE ENEMY

1.   Take authority over all the powers of darkness that rule in the place. Bind them with strong cords and keep them bound until God's purpose for the place has been accomplished.

2.   Bind in particular, the special satanic spirit that controls the other spirits that run the devil's errands in the place. Destroy the communication between the devil and all his servants in the spiritual realm.

3.   Release the glorious power of the Lord to rule in the town and make victorious spiritual battling possible.

LEADERSHIP

1.   Ask the Lord to raise up the right spiritual leadership for that town.

2.   Ask that the God-raised leadership would receive assurance from Him about their call to leadership.

3.   Demand that the Lord should grant to the leaders His eternal purpose for that place and His foreordained methods for realizing that purpose.

4.   Plead with the Lord that the leaders be given leadership gifts, including an unusual capacity to pick future leaders and train them.

THE LOCAL ASSEMBLY

Its Pattern and Ministry

1.   Ask the Lord that the local assembly be built on the pattern of the Lord as revealed in the New Testament and no other.

2.   Ask that its ministry be centered on the winning of sinners and establishing the saints.

Its Evangelism Ministry

1.   Lord, grant the Gospel to be proclaimed to all the sinners in the town by all the God-sanctioned methods, including personal evangelism by cassettes.

2.   Lord, grant those who hear the Gospel to repent and believe the whole Gospel.

3.   Lord, grant all the disciples to become members of the local church.

Its Teaching Ministry

1. Lord, raise up a teaching ministry for young converts.
2. Grant spiritually qualified teachers for the young convert's meetings.
3. Lord, raise up a deep and far-reaching teaching ministry for maturing saints.
4. Raise up teachers with teaching gifts for a lasting teaching ministry.
5. Reveal to the teachers how best to teach your Word so that it is understood and the right fruits borne for Your glory.
6. Create a deep hunger in the hearts of all Your children for the Word and grant them spiritual receptivity.
7. Lord, may some of those who are now being taught rapidly grow into teachers.

Its Prayer Life

1. Lord, make it into a praying church.
2. Grant their praying to be goal-directed.
3. Grant them to run a prayer strategy for the church and carry it out.
4. Raise up some of them into "watchmen."
5. May fasting become part of their normal prayer life.
6. Answer multitudes of their prayers as a token of Your love for them.

Its Life of Fellowship

1. Lord, may they be open and transparent to each other.
2. Lord, enable brotherly love to start and continue in all holiness.

3. Give them a spirit of mutual forgiveness and mutual submission.

4. Give them the ability to freely share with each other what they have received from You of both spiritual and material blessings.

5. Give them an unusual capacity to seek backsliders and restore them to the Lord.

Its Ministries

1. Raise ministers for every ministry in the local church.

2. Grant the ministers to be endued with spiritual power and authority and the spiritual gifts to be evident.

3. Enable their character to promote the Gospel.

THE WORLD

1. Bind and bring to naught all the attractive things of the world that aim at keeping sinners away from the Lord.

2. Create a deep dissatisfaction in the hearts of the unbelievers and cause them to seek the Lord and live.

3. Grant your children favour before the political and social leaders of the town so that the Gospel will not suffer setbacks.

FURTHER OUTREACH

1. Ask that the work be enabled to expand from this town to the other towns around so that Christ may be glorified.

2. Ask God to enable the daughter assemblies to stand mature in Christ.

PRAYING FOR A TOWN WITH DISCIPLES BUT WITHOUT A   LOCAL ASSEMBLY

1. Thank the Lord for enabling the existing disciples to be won to His Son.

2. Ask the Lord to provide someone to baptize them into water.

3. Ask the Lord to baptize all the disciples into the Holy Spirit.

4. Ask the Lord to provide a mature believer, full of the Holy Spirit to co-operate with the Holy Spirit and have the meetings of the local assembly started.

5. Ask the Lord to give all the disciples a spirit of oneness as the local assembly is started.

6. Ask the Lord to raise up someone with spiritual depth to visit the disciples regularly even as the apostle Paul and the others did in the New Testament.

7. Ask the Lord to open doors into the whole town so that it can be penetrated with the Gospel.

8. Ask the Lord to grant the disciples favour before the administrative and political leaders of the town.

9. Ask the Lord to hasten the day when it would become a fully established local assembly.

10. Ask the Lord to grant the mother assembly to faithfully watch and pray until these things are accomplished.

PRAYING FOR A MEETING OF FASTING INTERCESSORS

EXTERNAL FACTORS

1. Lord, grant weather conditions that will enhance the meeting in every way.

2. Lord, provide transportation for each one coming to the meeting so that no one will be kept away for lack of transportation.

3. Lord, grant each fasting intercessor to be able to get to the meeting-place in time so that the Lord may not be kept waiting for the prayers of His children.

ATTENDANCE

1. Lord, increase the number of fasting intercessors by :

a. Touching the spiritual eyes of those who have not yet seen the vision of fasting intercession to see it and become totally involved.

b. Deliver those brethren who do not fast out of a love for food from the power of food.

c. Enable information about fasting intercession to reach would-be fasting intercessors who at the moment do not know about the ministry.

THE FAST

1. Lord, take way all abnormal desire for food from all who are fasting.

2. Lord, renew the physical strength of fasting intercessors each Wednesday.

3.   Lord, make the Wednesday fast one of rejoicing for each of
your children.

THE PRAYER-MEETING

1.   Lord, grant to each fasting intercessor a spirit of expectancy
so that each will look forward to the meeting each Wednesday.

2.   Lord, take away the spirit of routine that could turn the meeting into a religious organization.

3.   Lord, grant a burden of prayer to each one present so that
he will find the prayer-meeting wonderful and thereby discharge his burden.

PHYSICAL ALERTNESS

1. Lord, grant each fasting intercessor physical alertness during
the prayer meeting so that:

a. Weakness in any form will be taken away.

b. Sleep may be taken away.

c. All physical distractions will be removed.

SPIRITUAL ALERTNESS

1.   Lord, grant each intercessor spiritual alertness by ensuring
that:

a. Each one is totally involved (body, soul, and spirit) during
the full length of the intercession.

b. None will go away without praying.

c. All forms of spiritual distraction are taken away.

THE PRAYER

1.   Lord, grant each prayer offered at the meeting to be:
   a.   Deep.
   b.   Fervent.
   c.   Intense.
   d.   Coherent.
   e.   Victorious.

THE LEADER

1.   Lord, grant the leader of each intercessory group to have a vision of the work and a vision of the world for which Christ died.

2.   Lord, reveal the mind of Christ about Cameroon to each leader.

3.   Lord, grant the leader to develop a deep prayer life in private.

4.   Lord, lay the burden of the ministry of Fasting Intercessors on their hearts so that it would claim their priority in prayer.

5.   Lord, grant each leader to take time to pray at home and prepare before the Lord.

THE END

1.   Lord, grant each one to leave the prayer-meeting fulfilled and full of praise, looking forward with expectation for the next meeting.

Praying for an Evangelistic Campaign - Before the Campaign

KEY DECISIONS

1. Lord, grant that the purpose of organizing the campaign be solely for the bringing of sinners to a saving knowledge for the Lord Jesus and for that purpose alone.

2. Lord, destroy any desire to organize the campaign for evangelism for:

    a. The promotion of a denomination

    b. The promotion of a movement

    c. The promotion of an individual or groups of individuals.

    d. The promotion of a particular doctrine.

    e. The opposition of a denomination, movement, individual, or doctrine.

    f. The display of talents, spiritual gifts, spiritual power, or even Christ.

    g. The display of self in any way whatsoever.

    h. The impression of some visitors or the entertainment of the public.

    i. The raising of funds either from the people present or by using the campaign as a tool of propaganda in order to raise funds abroad.

3. Lord, may the organizers be people who can discern your voice. May they only organize that campaign with full assurance that you would have them do it and not out of a spirit of carnal activity.

4. Lord, reveal the town or village or place where you want the campaign to be held so clearly that there will not be any doubts whatsoever.

5.   Lord, may Your children receive from You the dates of the campaign, and may they be sensitive to the Holy Spirit for any changes that He may want to bring in.

6.   Lord, show clearly the person You have chosen to be the evangelist at that particular campaign and protect him from the criticisms that result from the jealousy of the Church or the world.

7.   Show clearly at what hour of the day the meetings should begin.

8.   Lord, show clearly who should lead the team of people organizing the campaign.

9.   Lord, may each one who is given some responsibility be Your own choice for that task. Take away any desire to distribute responsibilities on the basis of:

   a. Tribe

   b. Education

   c. Physical appearance.

   d. Mere natural gifts.

   e. Religious politics.

Grant., Father, Your children to choose only on the assurance that it is Your man for the Job.

PRACTICAL PREPARATION

Authorizations

1. Lord, enable the application for the permit to hold the campaign to be written well ahead of time and cause it to be granted well ahead of time without any complications whatsoever.

2. Lord, enable the application to use the proposed site to be written well ahead of time and grant it to be granted without any problems whatsoever.

Publicity

1. Lord, provide a group of believers with the ability for publicity to handle the publicity of the campaign.

2. Lord, enable the campaign to be published on the radio and in many newspapers.

3. Lord, enable the banners to be well-produced and placed at strategic places.

4. Father, protect them from being destroyed by any instrument of the devil, be it man or wind or any other.

5. Lord, enable posters to be produced in the right quantity and placed in the right places.

6. Lord, enable thousands of handbills to be produced and distributed under the special leading and guidance of the Holy Spirit.

7. Lord, grant your children to make personal invitations by visiting hundreds of homes with invitations and explanations as to what the campaign is about.

8. Lord, grant the news of the campaign to spread to neighbouring towns and villages and draw many hungry people to the campaign.

9. Lord, in your wondrous sovereignty, grant all who are hungry for Christ to hear about the campaign.

10. Lord, protect the information about the campaign in people's hearts so that the Enemy will not snatch it away and thus cause them to forget.

Funds

1. Lord, provide all the funds that are needed for the campaign through those who belong to You and who love You and are concerned for the lost.

2. Forbid it, Lord, that any one be coaxed or forced to give so that His gift comes unwillingly.

3. Lord, grant to Your children to use the funds prayerfully and carefully as people who will have to give account to You about their use on that Day.

4. Lord, meet the financial needs for all the saints and sinners whom you have invited to the campaign.

5. Lord, show clearly how any funds that are left over after the campaign should be used in order to bring the greatest glory to Your name.

OTHERS

1. Lord, provide all the chairs and tables needed for the campaign.

2. Lord, provide appropriate places for those ministering in song.

3. Lord, enable the electrification of the place to be well done.

4. Lord, provide all the necessary items needed for the public-address system and keep the whole system protected under the blood of the Lord throughout the campaign.

5. Lord, provide a good place for the book ministry.

SPIRITUAL PREPARATION

1. Lord, grant the whole church to give herself without reservation to spiritual warfare in prayer for each aspect of the campaign.

2. Lord, enable the church to pray:

    a. Individually and informally.

    b. Individually and in an organized way with special hours, days, and weeks given to prayer.

c. Together and informally.

d. Together in an organized way with special periods, days, and weeks being given to heaven-storming and hell-destroying prayer.

Holiness

1. Lord, create in Your children a new hatred for sin and a new love for the holiness of God so that there will be nothing in their lives to limit the move of God.

2. Grant Your children to so seek You so as to be delivered from all weights, tendencies, et cetera which may appear innocent but which cause even the slightest leak in spiritual power.

3. Lord, prevent the Enemy from causing any major crisis in Your Body which will seriously impair the success of the campaign.

4. Lord, grant the holiness of Your children to include mutual love for each other, mutual encouragement, and a common vision and desire to see you glorified. Take away all divisions that the Enemy may want to bring in.

Praying for the Unbelievers

1. Lord, by Your Holy Spirit, sow a thirst and a hunger after God in the hearts of unbelievers before the date of the campaign.

2. Father, grant many unbelievers to come to the end of themselves to be disgusted with sin and hate it desperately and so desire to be delivered from its consequences ant its power.

3. Lord, move in a special way and open the eyes of the unbelievers that they may see the world's glory for what it is, i.e. transient and fading and so hate it.

4. Father, O that they would see Your glory for what it is – deep and permanent – and so desire it with all their hearts.

5. Lord, bring unbelievers to the campaign in their multitudes. Destroy any plans of the Enemy to keep them away. Particularly, Lord, ensure that he will not keep them away by:

    a. Sending them invitations to some other meetings taking place at the same time as the evangelistic campaign.

    b. Sending them out of the station for sudden business.

    c. Making them sick in body during the period of the campaign.

    d. Making them forget or confuse the dates.

    e. Making them suspect and misjudge the purpose of the campaign.

6. Lord, by the power of the Holy Spirit we release the unbelievers from the following chains of the devil: unbelief, a religious spirit, sorcery, magic, idolatry, fear, passivity, self-righteousness, and all that will stand in his way of understanding.

7. Lord, draw unbelievers in large numbers into the Kingdom of Your Son.

THE MESSAGE

1. Father, give the evangelist the messages that will be preached at the campaign.

2. Father, grant the messages to be Christ-centered and particularly Cross-centered.

3. Father, grant the messages to be simple and clear for all to understand.

4. Lord, may they place the unbelievers on trial.

5. Lord, grant them to clearly show Jesus crucified, risen, glorified, and soon coming as the only answer from You for man's sin and his lost state.

6. Lord, grant the message to speak to the unbelievers as individuals.

7. Lord, grant it to convict, convince, and convert many.

8. Lord, write the message clearly on the hearts and minds of all who hear it in such a way they will never be able to forget it even if they try very hard to do so.

THE MESSENGER (EVANGELIST)

1. Lord, make the reality of hell become clear in a totally different way to him and open his eyes to see as never before the horror of a Christless eternity. May these truths affect his message and ministry in a far-reaching way.

2. Lord, reveal to him the value of a soul.

3. Lord, open his eyes in a new way to see the seriousness of the evangelist's ministry and its evaluation by God.

4. Father, grant him to see in a new way Your love for sinner, and grant him to love them as You do.

5. Father, grant to your servant to know in a new way how to travail in prayer so that souls are won into the Kingdom of Your dear Son.

6. Lord, transform him into a man who only stands to preach after he has won the battle for souls on his knees.

7. Lord, grant him to receive the message from You, think about it, develop it, present it back to You, receive Your anointing upon it, and then go out and preach it to sinners.

8. Father, since Your power only flows with full force through a clean vessel, make Your servant pure and spotless so that he will be a channel through which Your message can flow unlimited and unhindered.

9. Lord, may Your Spirit rest upon him in a very special way during the entire campaign.

10. Lord, fill him with Your boldness and authority as he preaches Your Word.

11. Father, give him Your own sensitivity so that he will move with the Holy Spirit, being sharp and hard towards sin while being loving and tender towards the sinner.

12. Lord, make him so close to You and to the audience that he will know where to lay emphasis and when to stop.

13. Lord, grant him special guidance on how to make the invitation for sinners to respond to Your love. May the invitation come so clearly from You through him that sinners will forget the messenger and just hear You say to them, "Come to me."

14. Lord, fill him again and refresh him in preparation for further ministry.

DURING THE CAMPAIGN (THE ACTUAL MEETING)

GENERAL

1. Lord, bring all the people to each meeting on time, both believers and unbelievers.

2. Lord, control the weather so that the meeting, will be unhindered by rain or excess heat.

3. Overrule in the way people sit so that the believer will sit next to the unbeliever over whom he is able to exert the right spiritual influence.

4. Lord, may there be a special flow of life from Your children so that there will be an overall ministry of life in the whole meeting, not only from the speakers, but from all who are present.

5.   May the flow of life be maintained from the beginning of each meeting right through to its end.

6.   Lord, just be present in Your totality – Father, Son and Holy Spirit - and control everything happening.

The Leader

1.   Lord, grant him a good time of preparation during the week in preparation by prayer, fasting, and waiting on the Lord.

2.   Lord, guide him in the preparation of the programme.

3.   Lord, grant him to minister life as he leads.

4.   Lord, may he be so close to You that Your Holy Spirit will control the meeting through his spirit.

5.   Lord, lead him in the choice of songs and the person to lead each song so that the singing will minister to You and Your Body.

6.   Lord, help him to apportion the time rightly to each part of the campaign.

Testimonies

1.   Lord, grant each testimony to result from a desire to glorify the eternal Father, and that there will be no room for self-exhibition on self-glorification.

Counselling

1.   Lord, grant each counsellor to prepare specially for the campaign by much fasting and prayer and therefore be in very deep fellowship with the Lord of the harvest.

2.   Lord, may they each draw abundantly from You so that they will be able to minister out of this abundance to those they will counsel.

3. Lord, overrule in the pairing of counsellor and counselee so that they fit and can be ministered to spiritually.

4. Lord, may each counsellor be radiant and joyful and may each possess and manifest a very deep love for those they are counselling.

5. Lord, grant them to each lean on the Mighty Counsellor, the Holy Spirit as they counsel.

6. Lord, grant freedom between the one counselling and the one being counselled.

7. Lord, give each counsellor an unusual capacity to listen and to discern not only what is being said, but also what is not being said that should be said.

8. Lord, enable each counsellor to give himself away as life from You to the one being counselled.

9. Lord, grant to the counsellor a capacity to be sharp and tender as the need may demand.

10. Lord, enable the counsellor to discern who is ready to receive You and so lead him to You, and to know who is not ready and to let him go so that no premature spiritual births take place.

11. Lord, give the counsellor the same joy that angels in heaven possess over one sinner who repents, when the one being counselled receives You and is born again.

12. Lord, grant the counsellor a special love for the young convert that will enable him to labour in prayer and by all other ways until the young convert is presented to You, mature in Christ.

Praying for the Ministry of Song

PREPARATION (PRACTICE)

1. Lord, grant each person in the ministry to have been called into it personally and by You.

2. Lord, grant an overriding purpose for the ministry which will leave no room for any other purpose.

3. Lord, take away any desire to sing for fleshy reasons like self-display, human applause, et cetera.

4. Lord, provide good weather for the practice days.

5. Lord, grant each one going to the practice meeting to find transport easily and on time.

6. Lord, grant each singer to be able to get to the practice place on time so that the other singers are not kept waiting.

7. Lord, unite all of them, giving them the same mind and the same thoughts so that the Enemy will have no opportunity to interfere.

8. Lord, weld them into a team of lovers who love You and love each other dearly.

9. Lord, grant them Your intelligence so that they will learn the songs quickly and retain the words easily.

10. Lord, grant each practice session to be a festival of rejoicing and blessing so that they will look forward to it with spiritual eagerness.

11. Lord, grant each practice session to be preceded and followed by deep prayer at the personal level.

12. Lord, protect the musical instruments under the blood of the lamb and grant special ability to those playing the instruments so that they will continue to improve on their techniques and performance.

13. Lord, raise up more people and grant other instruments so that the volume and quality of praise by instruments that come to you will increase.

14. Lord, lead them by Your gentle Spirit in the choice of songs to be prepared for the following performance and grant them unity about the songs.

15. Lord, grant them a spirit of mutual submission each to the other and to the leaders who have been placed by the Body to direct them.

THE PERFORMANCE

1. Lord, may the entire performance be in the power of the Holy Spirit for the glory of Christ.

2. Lord, may their voices be at their best and may the words come out with such clarity that the audience will understand the meaning of the songs.

3. Lord, may the message of the songs carry in itself converting and transforming power.

4. Lord, may the physical appearance of the singers and their whole stage posture testify to the God who saw everything that He had made and its was "very good."

5. Lord, liberate each singer completely (body, soul, and spirit) so that they will give themselves away as they sing.

6. Lord, grant the audience to understand the words of the songs and not be carried away with just the melody.

7. Lord, keep your ministers humble to that they will not be carried away carnally by the applause of men.

8. Lord, keep the whole performance protected under the blood of Jesus so that the Enemy will have no access to it whatsoever.

AFTER THE CAMPAIGN

Praying for the Young Converts

1. Lord, enable the young convert to find a local assembly where You are worshipped as Lord and where Your Word is proclaimed without fear or favour and fully participate in it.

2. Lord, grant him a great thirst and hunger for Your Word, such as will cause him to do all that is possible to feed on the Word.

3. Lord, sow a deep love for You into his heart and teach him how to pray.

4. Lord, enable him to terminate clearly with the past and carry out the necessary restitution.

5. Lord, enable him to testify to the change that You have carried out in his life and not to be shy or ashamed of You.

6. Lord, lead him to be baptized into water and then baptize him into the Holy Spirit and give him spiritual gifts.

7. Lord, open his eyes to see what the world is, cause him to be separated from it and from all that it offers and be set apart entirely for You.

8. Lord, protect him from false doctrines.

9. Lord, grant him to abide and be mature in You until You come again.

10. Lord, enable his witness for You to bear fruit.

11. Lord, provide someone in the local assembly who is older and mature who will guide him and help him as he establishes roots in You.

12. Lord, supply all his needs - spiritual, intellectual, psychological, physical, and material – out of your treasury.

Praying for Those Who were Convicted but not Yet Converted

1. Lord, do not give them up but continue to woo them no Yourself.

2. Lord, enable them to have another opportunity to hear the Gospel and believe.

Praying for Those Who Came to the Campaign but Hardened their Hearts.

1. Lord, have mercy on them and do not harden their hearts.

2. Lord, because You died on the Cross for them, go out of Your way to grant faith to their faithless hearts.

Praying for the Local Assembly

1. Lord, may the local assembly be blessed in every way as a result of the campaign.

2. Lord, may the campaign result in the formation of new house churches for Your glory.

CHAPTER 15

Some practical issues with regard to prayer

TIME

The Bible recommends that we are to pray without ceasing, pray all the time, every possible minute. This must be the case in a normal life. However, prayer is more than these continuous contacts with God. It is very serious business. The Lord Jesus went aside every day, a long while before dawn, and prayed. He must have prayed during the day, but the morning was a special time of concentration in prayer. There must be special times of the day given to prayer.

The psalmist prayed in the morning. He said, *"But I, O Lord, cry to Thee; in the morning my prayer comes before Thee" (Psalms 88:13). "O Lord, in the morning Thou dost hear my voice; in the morning I prepare a sacrifice for Thee and watch"* (Psalm 5:3). *"I rise before dawn and cry for help"* (Psalm 119:147). He also prayed in the evening and at noon. He said, *"Evening and morning and noon I utter my voice"* (Psalm 55:17). *"Let my prayer be counted as incense before Thee, and the lifting up of my hands as an evening sacrifice"* (Psalm 141:2).

The apostles gave themselves to prayer. They had special times for prayer. The Bible says, *"Now Peter and John were going up to the temple at the hour of prayer, the ninth hour"* (Acts 3:1). *"The next day, as they were on their journey and coming near the city, Peter went up on the housetop to pray, about the sixth hour"* (Acts 10:9). *"But about midnight Paul and Silas were, praying and singing hymns to God, and the prisoners were listening to them"* (Acts 16:25).

Every believer should prayerfully seek God's face and obtain from the Lord that time in the day that he sets aside for prayer. Once that is done, that time must be jealously guarded from the intrigues of the Enemy, for he will do everything possible to attack it. This will mean that we are prepared to leave everything else aside when that hour comes so that we may pray. Sometimes we will have to act in a way that people may misunderstand us, but it is better to be misunderstood than to miss an appointment with God. When we have fixed a certain time for prayer, that time will become a daily appointment with God. We must keep our own side of the appointment for God will certainly keep His, and it would be unfair to keep Him waiting. This calls for discipline, but are we not called to be disciples? Disciples are disciplined people.

In addition to the daily times for prayer, which for the normal believer will be a daily one or two hours with God in personal prayer, we need to plan some longer periods of prayer. The Lord Jesus had a personal all-night meeting before He choose the twelve apostles. We too should plan personal all-night prayer-meetings. We should in addition plan prayer weekends. That is, we should plan and go away for a weekend for the purpose of praying and there spend the time in prayer.

What of seasons of prayer? This is wonderful. This means that we take, say, a month and consecrate it to prayer. We may couple it with fasting for greater efficacy.

PLACES OF PRAYER

The Lord Jesus continually withdrew to a lonely place and there He prayed. He sought for a place where He could concentrate and He wanted to draw the attention of God and not that of men. The Lord also recommended that prayer should be a secret affair, "*And when you pray, you must not be like hypocrites, for they love to stand and pray in the synagogues and at the street corners, that they may be seen by men. Truly, I say to you, they have their reward. But when you pray, go into your room and shut the door and pray to your Father who is in secret; and your Father who sees in secret will reward you*" (Matthew 6:5-6).

I suggest that each saint should select some quiet place where he goes regularly to fight the good fight of faith in prayer. We are not suggesting that he should not pray in other places. We, however, recommend that when someone sets a week-end aside for the Lord, he should withdraw to some quiet place and there pray. Such a place will become in some special way his special place for meeting God.

Of course, we cannot wait to be in such places for the daily time of prayer with the Lord, nor can we do that in emergencies. Jeremiah prayed from the low dungeon (Lamentation 3:55) and Jonah prayed from the fish's belly, and God heard them.

Permit me to share with you an experience of one of the sisters in our local assembly which brought a lot of joy to my heart. She is about twenty-two years of age and has known the Lord for about two years. Her ambition is to love the Lord without the slightest reservation. She had three weeks of leave from her job and she came to me to ask me what were the pressing needs of the church that needed to be attended to in prayer. I gave her a list of prayer topics. She then withdrew to some quiet place on a hilltop where she spent two weeks and five days, eating one light meal a day and praying for the interests of the Lord in Cameroon. She must have ministered life to the Body of Christ. Our prayer is that many in the Church will know the same level of withdrawal and abandonment to the Lord for the business of prayer. Lord Jesus, may what she did become the normal and not remain the exception in Your Church.

POSTURE IN PRAYER

At least, five different postures were used by the praying men of the Bible.

STANDING

"*And when all the people saw the pillar of cloud standing at the door of the tent, all the people would rise up and worship, every man at his tent door"* (Exodus 33:10), *"Then Solomon stood before the altar of the Lord in the presence of all the assembly of Israel, and spread forth his hands towards heaven and said, O Lord God of Israel..."* (2 Chronicles 6:12). *"If evil comes upon us by the sword, judgment, or pestilence, or famine, we will stand before this house, and before Thee, for Thy name is in this house, and cry to Thee in our affliction, and Thou wilt hear and save"* (2 Chronicles 20:9).

BOWING

"Then I bowed my head and worshipped the Lord, and blessed the Lord, the God of my master Abraham, who had led me by the right way..." (Genesis 24:48).   *"And Moses made hast to bow his head toward the earth, and worshipped"* (Exodus 34:8). *"Ezra blessed the Lord, the great God; and all the people answered, 'Amen, Amen,' lifting up their hands; and they bowed their heads and worshipped the Lord with their faces to the ground"* (Nehemiah 8:6).

SITTING

"Then King David went in and sat before the Lord, and said, 'Who am I, O Lord God, and what is my house that Thou has brought me thus far?'" (1 Chronicles 17:16).

KNEELING

"O come, let us worship and bow down, let us kneel before the Lord, our Maker!" (Psalm 95:6). *"Now as Solomon finished offering his prayer and supplication to the Lord, he arose from before the altar of the Lord, where he had knelt with hands outstretched toward heaven and he stood, and blessed all the assembly of Israel with a loud voice"* (1 Kings 8:54-55). *"And he knelt down and cried with a loud voice; 'Lord, do not hold this sin against them' "*(Acts 7:60). *"And when he had spoken thus, he knelt down and prayed with them all"* (Acts 20:36).   *"For this reason I*

bow my knees before the Father, from whom every family in heaven and on earth is named…" (Ephesians 3:14).

LYING DOWN

"Then Jehoshaphat bowed down his head with his face to the ground, and all Judah and the inhabitants of Jerusalem fell down before the Lord, worshipping the Lord" (2 Chronicles 20:18).

So, there are varied postures that can be used during prayer. Holiness or success in prayer does not depend on the posture. They depend on the heart condition of the praying man. Posture is not a permanent thing that one assumes. During the same period of prayer, it is often possible to stand and then sit and then kneel. I personally adopted a walking position. When I have to pray for the needs of one believer after another, sometimes late at night I often walk as I talk to the Lord. That helps me to concentrate. We should let the Holy Spirit guide us as to what posture to assume in prayer.

WITH OR WITHOUT NOISE

Many people wonder whether or not they are to pray aloud or silently. First of all, in a meeting where there are other believers, the voice level has to be such that all who are present can hear you so as to be caught up with you in prayer. It is very disturbing in a prayer-meeting to have someone whisper silently to the Lord and yet expect other to be involved with him in prayer. On the other hand, some people scream at God so loudly that it disturbs others from concentrating in prayer. God is not deaf. He is not asleep so that we need to shout Him out of it. At a prayer-meeting the volume must be such as to enable others to participate unhindered.

During one's private prayer, is one to pray silently or aloud? The Bible has no rules. The Bible says, *"Hearken to the sound of my cry, my King and my God, for to Thee do I pray. O Lord, in the morning Thou dost hear my voice; in the morning I prepare a sacrifice for Thee and watch"* (Psalms 5:2-3). Hannah prayed but not audibly. Whether we pray aloud or silently poses no problem to God. He will hear both prayers. However, many people have found out that praying aloud helps them to concentrate better. Intensity in prayer is not directly related to noise or the absence of it. Let us always remember this, for some use loud tones to try to impress others of a nonexistent spirituality.

WITHOUT WORDS

There is a place in the communion between man and God in prayer where words are not necessary. The human spirit reaches out to God so much so that spiritual impressions are made on God directly, without the use of the intermediary of words. The psalmist was expressing something of this when he said, "Teach me the way I should go, for to Thee I lift up my soul" (Psalm 143:8). *"To Thee, O Lord, I lift up my soul O my God, in Thee I trust"* (Psalm 25:1).

At such moments there may be only groans or sobs or some expression of the being flowing out unconsciously to the Lord. Praying in this way is not something that one reads and tries to imitate what someone is talking about. It is something into which the gracious Holy Spirit leads us, slowly and steadily.

A PRAYER PARTNER

Although the Lord Jesus often withdrew to be alone with God in prayer, we notice that He also often desired the close companionship of those who were closest to Him. The Bible says, *"Now*

*about eight days after these sayings He took with Him Peter and John and
James and went up on the mountain to pray"* (Luke 9:28).   *"Then Jesus went with them to a place called Gethsemane and He said to His disciples, 'Sit here, while I go yonder and pray.'   And taking with Him Peter and the two sons of Zebedee, He began to be sorrowful and troubled.
The He said to them, 'My Soul is very sorrowful, even to death; remain
here and watch with me"'*   (Matthew 26:36-38).

I want to suggest that there are places in the climbing of the spiritual ladder in prayer that we need the companionship of another
human being with us for victory. There are points beyond which we
will not be able to go without another praying soul with us. I cannot explain the theory well, but I know it from deep experience. Permit me to share with you something that I experienced not too long
ago. The Lord told me that every provincial headquarters, divisio-
nal headquarters, subdivisional headquarters, and all towns of
consequence were to be interceded for, in a most serious way, in order to break down the advancing forces of the Enemy and provide,
in prayer, the preliminary background of prayer for the move of
God in national evangelization which was to come later on.   He also
made it clear that I would not be equal to the task alone. After prayer
and some reflection, I invited two other believers with whom I had
much liberty in prayer.

It was mighty wrestling as we divided our country into nine "spiritual provinces" and took each province in turn: writing down the
names of all towns and villages of any consequence (from a recent
map) and then wrestling through for four to six hours each night,
five nights a week for five weeks. At some points the battle was so
fierce that although we were three and occasionally four, we felt like
fainting and breaking down. It was only the special anointing of the
Lord and sustaining energy from each other that enabled us to press
on until the task was accomplished. I could never have accomplished that task alone, at least not at this stage in my spiritual pilgrimage.

During this particular time of special intercession, when the battle was so fierce and the Enemy resisting the breakdown of his strongholds, we would use the authority of the Church to force him to obey. It was wonderful that I was not alone. We had been gathered, brought together by the Lord for a special purpose, and being three, He was both in us and in our midst. If I were alone, He would have been in me and not in my midst. The Lord said, *"For where two of there are gathered in my name, there am I in the midst of them"* (Matthew 18:20).

A prayer partner is someone with whom you have extraordinary liberty in prayer, love and respect, as well as trust. He must be someone before whom you can be thoroughly transparent, being able and willing to share your deepest thoughts, yearnings, and failures. He should be someone with a like passion for the Lord as you, a person committed to prayer, who will enhance your prayer life. He should also be available for frequent and much prayer.

The Lord Jesus said, *"Again I say to you, if two of you agree on earth about anything they ask, it will be done for them by my Father in heaven"* (Matthew 18:19).

Prayer partners must aim at enhancing the spiritual life of the local church and not allow the Enemy to put them away and use them to scatter the local assembly. If their praying is normal, a substantial portion of their praying would be for the blessing of the local church.

The question may arise in some hearts, Where can I find someone who can be my prayer partner? How can I find someone to whom I can completely open myself and not be let down? The answer is simple: Ask and it shall be given to you. Seek and you shall find. However, the number one thing – deep fellowship, as must exist between prayer partners - is a work of the Holy Spirit, but He works in hearts that are willing. Are you willing? The best way to another person's heart is by being open yourself to him. To the extent that you open yourself up to another and give yourself away, will that person, by the help of the Lord, come along the same path of openness and, often, brokenness.

PRAYER RECORDS

Prayer is serious business. It is taking sides with God in a transaction. We dare not take up an issue in prayer with God and then leave it unsettled. The experience of too many believers is that they take up an issue with God while it is pressing on their hearts. They pray about it for some time, and then they forget about it. This is very sad, and everything should be done to stop it. If, for example, the Lord laid it upon your heart to pray for the conversion of Mr. A and you start faithfully and soon forget about the whole matter, how do you expect the Lord to treat such a prayer? He is likely to do what you did – let it go altogether. For this reason, I suggest that each believer should keep a prayer record. There are many reasons why this will help the believer's prayer life. As can be seen from the suggested ruling of a prayer book, the number helps us to be organized. The date first prayed will help us to actually start praying about a certain issue instead of just wishing that we prayed. The date will also enable us to see how long we have been praying for that particular matter. The topic of prayer will enable us to know exactly what it is that we want to pray about. We will learn to be exact. The Bible backing will enable us to ensure that we are praying on the grounds of scripture and that we can reasonably expect God to fulfill His written Word by answering our prayers. The date on which the prayer was answered will help us to know that the particular issue at hand has been settled and that the Lord has answered. The manner of answering will help us to begin to see in a new way the ways by which God moves to answer our prayers. This will furthermore help us to pray precisely for any prayer topic which will not have an exact answer, which we can know for certain will not be recorded here.

The prayer record has further advantages. First of all, it enables the praying saint to give thanks to the Lord for answered prayers. We remember that God has answered this prayer and that one and the other one for which thanks should be given to Him. With an increasing number of answered prayers, we grow in faith; and the desire to pray is enhanced as we prove in an ever-increasing way the truth that "God answers the prayers of His children."

Secondly, the prayer record serves as an exhibit against the Enemy during times of severe trials, when he would tempt us to doubt God's goodness. At such times we can open our prayer record and read out loud to him many of the prayers that our God answered and like our Lord, tell him to depart from us. And depart he will.

Lastly, the prayer record can serve as an indicator to us to show us that something is out of tune in our relationship with God. If we should go through a period when days, weeks, and even months should pass by without obvious answers to definite prayers, how are we to take that? It will certainly say that a cloud has come between us and our heavenly Father, that we have grieved the Holy Spirit and that we ought to seek His face at once so as to be told what the matter is.

Personally, I have four prayer notebooks. The first one is of preliminary nature. I write issues that come to my mind as possible issues for prayer. The possible subjects of prayer remain there while I seek God's will as to whether or not it is His will that I make such a subject a matter of definite prayer. After some time I will know God's will about the matter. After that, if it is not God's will, I will just cross out the matter. If it is His will, then the matter will be recorded in one of three possible notebooks, depending on what it is.

Notebook 1 is shown at the end of this book, where prayer request is specific and for which definite answers are possible.

Notebook 2 is for definite prayer topics, but prayers whose answers are more difficult to define. For example, I would record prayer topics about the growth of the local assembly in purity and power and continue to pray about this without one day feeling that the prayer is finally answered, although there would be indications that God is answering the prayer. Another would be a prayer request that I would grow in the knowledge of our Lord and Saviour, a prayer request that, though definite, will continue to be prayed until we meet the Lord in the air.

Notebook 3 contains prayers for specific people. Many people ask me to pray for them or the Holy Spirit reveals the need to pray for them to me. Of the people related to me, either in the family or in the ministry, there may be many topics from or concerning one person. Instead of just scattering them here and there, depending on the dates in which the topics came up, I decided to have the third notebook, where I devote a page or more to one person or to the issue. In that way when I want to pray for brother E or sister P, I open to the page(s) where his needs are and pray.

The question may be asked, How do you go about praying over the topics in the various books, especially when they reach their thousands in numbers? This is what I do. I have set some time in each day for each of the prayer books. I just start from number one and I may stop at number fifteen. If the topic has been answered I give thanks to the Lord. I mark out the fact that I stopped at number fifteen and the next day I continue from number sixteen and go on until I come to the last recorded topic and then I start all over.

Of course, all my prayer time is not spent with the notebooks before me. There are times of waiting before the Lord during which the Holy Spirit will lead differently in prayer. Nevertheless, I have found an organized prayer life useful.

PROMISES MADE BUT NEVER FULFILLED?

Anyone with some standing in the Church of the Lord Jesus, especially when he leads part of the Church of some size, will often have people coming to him with prayer requests. Mr. X may bring two or three requests, Mrs Y may bring three or four, and Miss Z may bring two, all in one. The person to whom the prayer requests are brought will in all probability promise to pray for theses people and for those subjects. He may then move to another place where other people will present their needs to him. If his memory is good or better than a taper recorder, he will remember all these names and requests and pray about them. If his memory is not so retentive, he will forget some of the people and their requests. He would then not pray for them and therefore commit the sin of lying. I wonder how many people commit this sin in the realm of unfulfilled promises to pray and yet carry themselves about as if they have not sinned at all? Does God take it so lightly? Is it right before God and before man to betray the trust of a little one of God by such carelessness?

I see only one way of overcoming this grievous sin – record the prayer request. Be organized in prayer. A good but poorly organized business will not reach its maximum potential. A deep but poorly organized prayer life will also fail to realize its fullest potential. Will you do something about organizing your prayer life? Start now!!

No	Date prayed	Topic of prayer	Bible baking	Answered date	How answered
001	07.06.1981	Lord, save our son Paul	Acts 16:31	14.01.83	He gave his life to the Lord Jesus
002	07.06.1981	Lord God, do you want the Jesus Festival to take place this year?	Psalm 32:8		